What Others Are Saying about this Book . . .

"Your extraordinary book has given me valuable insights . . . and I expect readers will agree." —**Spencer Johnson, M.D., co-author of** *The One Minute Manager* **and author of** *Who Moved My Cheese?*

"In this book, the author demonstrates that a universal principle is at work in places where one would hardly imagine it. Once introduced to the idea, I found myself seeing co-opetition everywhere. This is a gift to all who value simple, powerful ideas." — **David Bowles, Ph.D., co-author,** *The High Engagement Work Culture*

"As this brilliant book shows, the law of co-opetition allows the free magic of nature to light our way and simplify complex systems." —**Ted Gildred, former US Ambassador to Argentina**

A PRIMAL WISDOM

Nature's Unification of Cooperation
and Competition

Second Edition

V. Frank Asaro, JD

A corollary to the novel: *The Tortoise Shell Game,*
by V. Frank Asaro, J.D.

BETTIE YOUNGS BOOKS

Front cover design: Background, not including the canoe, is
from the image BESTLINES, by brilliant digital artist Ted Packman. The outrigger canoe, superimposed in the foreground as
part of cover design, is from canstockphoto.com.

Text Layout: Jane Hagaman

BETTIE YOUNGS BOOK PUBLISHERS
www.BettieYoungsBooks.com

If you are unable to order this book from your local bookseller
or online, or from wholesalers Baker & Taylor or Ingram, you
may order directly from the Publisher: sales@BettieYoungs.com.

Library of Congress Control Number is available upon request.

ISBN: 978-1-940784-55-7
Ebook ISBN: 978-1-940784-56-4

10 9 8 7 6 5 4 3 2 1

Contents

Setting the Stage

An Important Word
from the Author

In the late 1970s, I began writing essays about "co-opetition," a theory I had developed that unifies the apparently opposing behavioral forces of cooperation and competition. One might also describe it as cooperative competition or competitive cooperation.

The most important aspect of the theory was that such *unification* or synthesis—to use another word—uses certain laws of nature to simplify the workings of complex systems. I knew that this information would be valuable to anyone attempting to manage or perfect such systems—or any system. I also knew that the knowledge could help solve problems ranging from those involving personal relationships to social, economic, and political issues.

In 1990, after I circulated these essays and related notes in search of feedback, I was flattered to receive the following comments in a letter from noted writer Spencer Johnson, M.D., coauthor of the bestselling *The One Minute Manager*, he later also wrote the bestselling *Who Moved My Cheese?* He said, in part:

Your extraordinary notes . . . have given me some valuable insights. . . . I especially appreciate the way you have drawn an eclectic universe of knowledge from physics to anthropology and I expect many other appreciative readers will agree.

He urged me to expand the concept into a book, which I began to do while otherwise happily engaged in the practice of law. Over the years, I continued to send out manuscripts and discuss the theory with others; I even engaged university graduate students as researchers to test and verify the idea. They all came back enthusiastic about it.

Others have since used the word coopetition in their writings, especially in Game Theory in the business field, but no matter the realm to which it is applied, the principle remains the same— the unification, merger, or synthesis of cooperating and competing behaviors will help solve most problems of the world. You will now—as of 2015—find on Wikipedia extensive writings and references to the co-opetition theory, including the works of your gratified author. National television has picked up on the theory by an author interview on *Fox and Friends*, YouTube February 2013.

As you will see, this principle is drawn primarily from nature. In this context, what do we mean by "nature?" We're talking about everything from the force behind the workings of Adam Smith's "invisible hand" in economics to the sound of a beautiful chord in music. But nature does not favor perfect balance; as we'll discover, the "competition" part of "co-opetition" is nature's main emphasis.

We'll also find that locating the synthesis point between cooperation and competition in a system is largely an intuitive task—because synthesis itself is part of, and comes from, nature. This is the primal wisdom I wish you to recognize. After you've fully read this work you should know a great deal more about nature's magic and how to employ it.

In 2011, twenty-five or so years after I first wrote about the subject, I saw that the nation and world faced even more economic and political turmoil and polarization than when I first organized my theory. I believed it was crucial to get the word out on the general philosophy of co-opetition. The book Universal Coopetition, published in 2011, was the result. I novelized the theory in The Tortoise Shell Code, published in 2013, and have now optimized it in my novel, The Tortoise Shell Game, published in 2015 .

Many corollaries to the novel are depicted in this new non-fiction work, *A Primal Wisdom,* 2d ed. Although this current volume incorporates all the concepts presented in Universal Coopetition, the current book is entirely up-dated and over one-third longer than the original. It should be regarded as a second edition, superseding Universal Coopetition.

Over the years, I've generated the axioms set forth below. I offer them now with the hope that a reading of this book will make clear their full meanings:

"Life would be so much easier if we'd just leave some room for nature to work her magic."

"When Earth no longer suffers from earthquakes, tsunamis, and volcanoes, human life will die."

"Finding the asymmetric balance of the ultimate synthesis, is a primal wisdom."

"Nature will assist in managing complex systems, if only we would let her do her work."

"When giving happens spontaneously through altruism, empathy, and goodness of heart, such is a testament to the humanity of human kind, but when it is forced through government mandate it is testimony to the tyranny that can envelop humankind."

V. Frank Asaro—2015

1

The Idea

The term "co-opetition" is, of course, a combination of the nouns "cooperation" and "competition." But it is more than just a portmanteau of those two word—it embodies, in fact, the very concept it describes: the synthesis of opposing forces into a single dynamic. The resulting fusion is, among many other things, an antidote to extreme polarization.

Co-opetition allows nature herself to help people effortlessly and intuitively simplify a system—any system—especially one that's monstrously complex. Letting nature work her magic is both an art and an act of wisdom. In this book we will learn to use this primal wisdom of nature.

Cooperation and competition. Giving and taking. Benevolence and self-interest. We all have within us the many opposing impulses that comprise co-opetition. The problem is that if either extreme becomes overly dominant, the result tends to be bad, or even disastrous. This work endeavors to identify the natural point of fusion or synthesis—aka, the sweet spot—between cooperation and competition as it applies to various situations, and explain why doing so is critically important. Of course the concept has its greatest utility for the human being and the social animals, but It also has application to all other forms of life and systems.

Note that I refer to the natural point of fusion or synthesis. This book springs from my conviction that not only human beings, but animals and plants, art and music, politics and economics, geological formations, science and physics—in fact, everything in the universe—is inherently co-opetitive.

Why? Because the universe is itself inherently co-opetitive. And we are all made from the stuff of stars.

Allow me at this early point to stress a minor thing. If ever you feel any of the following invokes more pause to ponder than you have the time for, feel free to skim a little and retrace later; more meat and potatoes builds in the later chapters. In the early sections I wanted to create for you a solid foundation, important for better understanding the synthesis for *A Primal Wisdom.*

FOUR SLUGGERS AND A BICYCLE RACER

Before we get into full analysis of the concepts in this book, let me illustrate the importance of locating the best point, or fulcrum, of synthesis for a particular situation. It's also known as the sweet spot.

Consider a few great baseball players from both past and present: Ted Williams and Hank Aaron on the one hand; Barry Bonds and Alex Rodriguez on the other. We'll also take a brief look at bicycle racer Lance Armstrong. I'm not trying to single these athletes out in particular, for there are other numerous examples; they merely help illustrate a point.

Professional sports, in general, and baseball, in particular, represent the epitome of competition, but also depend very much on cooperation. Obviously, if you don't have rules that are agreed upon and adhered to by everyone, you have no sport—you have chaos.

Ted Williams grew up in the 1930s in San Diego, California, where he played unsupervised baseball as a kid under the lights of a small neighborhood community center. He had so much fun playing the game that they regularly had to shut the lights off to get him to go home. If you know baseball at all, you know the rest of this story. Williams became arguably the best hitter of all time, with the highest lifetime batting average ever at .344 and the highest single-year average of .406. He attained those statistics despite two interruptions in his sports career: when he served as an aviator in WWII and again in the Korean War. He received several medals as a jet fighter-pilot-war hero. He accomplished all this by virtue of talent, hard work, and relentless practice; performance-enhancing drugs had not yet been invented.

Hank Aaron, best known for hitting 755 lifetime home runs—passing Babe Ruth's record of 714—was born in 1934 and grew up in Mobile, Alabama. He played in 24 All-Star Games, and as of 2007 led the number of bases gained with 6,856. He won four Most Valuable Player awards, was named leader of the league in RBIs four times, the leader in home runs three times, and won the Golden Glove Award in 1974, among other accomplishments. And he did it all without resorting to performance enhancing drugs; talent, practice, and professionalism were his primary resources.

Barry Bonds was born in Riverside in southern California and grew up in San Carlos, California in the 1960s and 1970s. Bonds' accomplishments put him among the greatest baseball players who ever lived. This accolade is backed up by his record-setting seven Most Valuable Player awards—four of them bestowed in consecutive years (also a record)—along with his fourteen All-Star awards and eight Golden Gloves, not to mention his numerous Major League Baseball records. He holds the all-time home run record with 762, surpassing Hank Aaron, and is also the all-time career leader in both walks (2,558) and intentional walks (688). Bonds holds numerous other baseball records, including the single-season Major League home run record, set in 2001.

Alex Rodrigues, aka "A-Rod," a major-league shortstop and third baseman, was born in New York City and raised in the Dominican Republic and Miami, Florida. He's known as one of the best all-around baseball players to ever live. He was the 1996 American League batting champion. He set numerous records for doubles, matched total bases for a shortstop, led the American league in doubles, led the league in runs five times, and led his league in total bases three years. He was the best hitting shortstop seven seasons, an all-star five times, and held many other records awards.

Lance Armstrong was born on September 18, 1971, in Plano, Texas. At age 16, he became a professional triathlete; at 18 he trained as a cyclist with the U.S. Olympic development team and placed higher in the World Championship Road Race than any American since 1976. He went on to win seven consecutive Tour de France titles and to inspire multitudes with the true story of his miracle cancer survival.

TOO COMPETITIVE

But this is where the stories of these five professional athletes diverge. On April 13, 2011, a jury found Barry Bonds guilty on the felony charge of obstructing justice stemming from an investigation into his alleged use of performance-enhancing drugs. Although his first appeal was denied, he asked for reconsideration. In April 2015, the 9th Circuit Court threw out the conviction.

On August 5, 2013, Alex Rodriquez was suspended fifty games by the league for allegedly taking performance-enhancing drugs. After more than a year he had a stunning return to the game.

In 2012, Lance Armstrong was stripped of seven Tour de France titles due to doping charges.

The rule-making bodies in virtually all professional sports forbid the use of performance-enhancing drugs, which give athletes who take them advantages over athletes who rely strictly on training and their own physical and mental gifts. In other words, the use of performance enhancing drugs is considered "cheating"— stepping beyond the accepted, universal, cooperative rules of the game or sport. In this light, the history of record proves that the fusion point between cooperation and competition that Ted Williams and Hank Aaron chose was properly placed. They did not allow their competitive drive to overdrive into cheating. Cooperation with the rules kept competition under control. Co-opetition prevailed. But it appears from the actions taken by the officals that Barry Bonds, Alex Rodriguez, and Lance Armstrong each placed their points of fusion too far in the competition realm. If so, co-opetition failed, and the allegations that they gained unfair advantage through the use of drugs will likely always overshadow their career attainments. But what's more disheartening is the inevitable disillusionment of those who have been inspired by these heroes—inspired to fight their personal calamities, including cancer, as in Armstrong's example.

Some of them appear to have gained greater wisdom from their controversial experiences and are continuing forward brilliantly with their careers and aspirations.

Because competition compels people to seek advantage over their opponents, it is a realm especially rich with examples of unperfected co-opetition. However, it is equally possible, as we shall see, to place the point of synthesis too far on the side of cooperation.

TOO MUCH COOPERATION:
Buried in Good Fortune

In 1324 AD, King Mansa Musa, ruler of the city-state of Timbuktu—now one of the most remote and desolate areas in all of Africa—took a prodigious amount of gold with him on his pilgrimage to Mecca. From Timbuktu, he traveled north to Tripoli with eighty gold-laden camels, sixty thousand men, and twelve thousand slaves, covering a distance of more than twelve hundred miles—before proceeding east through Cairo.

Along the way, Musa freely handed out gold in the belief that he was cooperating with God for the benefit of His people. The closer he came to civilization, the more lavish his giving became, until by the time he arrived at Mecca he had entirely run out of gold.

The result? Musa distributed so much wealth that he destabilized the entire economy of the Egyptian region, and for the next ten years the people suffered the effects of super-inflation. By satisfying his noble goal of maximizing cooperation between himself and his people, Musa inadvertently destabilized and "competed" with the established workings of the market, money-changers, and gold merchants, resulting in the unintended consequence of ruining the economy of the entire region. The short-term benefit of his great generosity turned out to be vastly overshadowed by the long-term damage it caused. An aphorism comes to mind: "The road to hell is paved with good intentions."

In this case co-opetition failed because of too much cooperation of the "do-gooder" variety. History is replete with examples:

In the 1920s, certain groups in the United States thought it was a good idea to curtail alcohol-related "sins" by enacting Prohibition. That act, however, had the unintended consequence, among others, of leading to a wave of bootlegging, smuggling, and organized crime. One of the Godfather films colorfully depicted this era.

In Afghanistan during the years preceding 9/11, the CIA thought it was a good idea to fund and supply the Mujahedin with weapons. At the time, the Mujahedin were fighting the Soviet Union. But American support of the Mujahedin also led to Al Qaeda, Osama bin Laden, and the destruction of the World Trade Center in New York with the tragic deaths of almost five thousand people—not to mention the many more deaths and casualties that followed as a U.S.-led coalition went to war in Afghanistan, then Iraq.

During the administrations of presidents Carter, Bush Sr. and son, and Clinton—and with the later silent acquiescence of a young first term Democrat senator who later became president of the U.S.—the government did something else it thought was good: In 2005, it tried to "cooperate" with low-to middle-income home-buyers by continuing a program to help them buy homes, notwithstanding that in fact the result would be disastrous for them. The Senate closed its eyes when the Republican House and most of their colleagues in the Senate tried to pass a bill to audit the quasi-government agencies of Fannie Mae and Freddie Mac; those agencies were facilitating the financing of these high-risk home loans. The government had been operating a social engineering program to help low to moderate income residents become home owners—to own homes they otherwise could not afford. Years earlier, to promote this low income home ownership among other things, at President Clinton's urging Congress had expanded the Community Reinvestment Act ("CRA"), further promoting home ownership by the less privileged.

In approximately 2004, Fannie Mae and Freddy Mac were rumored to have been in deep financial trouble. Even as far back as 2000,there were strong indications that Fannie Mae and Freddie Mac were having financial problems because of this 'social engineering'policy. As said, most Republicans wanted them audited. The Democratic Senate along with a minority of Republicans would not take up the bill to do the audit.They refused even to vote on the audit bill. Three years later, it became clear that those quasi-government agencies of Fannie Mae and Freddie Mac had played a major part in the cause of the subprime mortgage bubble. The burst of that bubble triggered the financial debacle of the Great Recession of 2008. To implement the necessary home buyer-financing, the government had allowed "Fannie Mae" and "Freddie Mac" to "guaranty" –that is, to purchase the loan paper mortgages—from the home-lenders. As said, it was very risky loan paper.

In 2008, to its utter dismay and the shock of the economic world, Congress publically discovered that both Fannie and Freddie were many hundreds of billions of dollars upside down in debt. Silently, Congress probably already knew this. The agencies were put into conservatorships, and the U.S. Treasury had to bail them out—a daunting task indeed.

The result was the subprime mortgage financial debacle of 2008. This plunged not only the U.S. into the longest, deepest recession since the Great Depression of the early 1930s, but tsunamied the economies of the entire world.

Similar to the gold-lined trek of King Mansa Musa, the subprime mortgage fiasco is an example of too much "cooperation," as I use the term in this book. I will alternatively refer to this phenomenon as "uber-cooperation."

FINDING THE FULCRUM, THE SWEET SPOT

What should Musa have done differently? Or Barry Bonds and Lance Armstrong, or the CIA, or Congress? How does one determine where lies the best point of synthesis between competition and cooperation?

This book will illustrate the answer to that question with examples involving everything from wine-making to playing the piano, from playing politics to fathoming economics, from Roman history to the stars—even from making war to making peace.

As mentioned earlier, this work asserts that all of nature strives to locate and settle at that fulcrum point—the ultimate synthesis at which cooperation and competition are unified and appropriately distributed for any given situation. It's the human beings who cause unfortunate results when, for either selfish or altruistic reasons—or even because of plain old ignorance—they fail to accomplish the same task. They fail to find the ultimate synthesis. They fail to find the sweet spot within the equation of cooperative competition.

Theoretically, the most efficient possible operation of any system can be achieved by adjusting the placement of the fulcrum in the correct direction: between order and chaos, which means between cooperation and competition. Further, the position of the fulcrum, whether situated by mankind or by nature, must be set for the particular system being considered. There is no generic point of co-opetition.

Fortunately, the struggle to find synthesis, or the sweet spot, is for the most part intuitive and instinctive, a form of primal wisdom. But clearly this is not always the case. In the situation of athletes who are too competitive to a fault, perhaps the enforcers did not exercise sufficient "compulsory cooperation" to ensure that the competition was fair for all the athletes. Some individuals presumably got caught, but who knows how many cheaters slipped through the cracks?

It could be that most were cheating. In that case, what appears to be athletic competition is actually a competition about how good a cheater you are—because if you don't participate in the cheating, you'll never have a chance to win against those who do cheat. That's not fair either; it almost excuses the athletes who get caught. Thus, some of the fault lies with those who are supposed to enforce the rules: they must do their jobs well.

In general, however, we all recognize the appropriate point of synthesis when we find it; it becomes self-evident. Post hoc history will verify the accuracy of our choice.

When human beings achieve synthesis in any endeavor we can associate closely with one another for our common good while remaining individually separate and free. We can preserve our personal liberty while also living as social creatures.

An important finding about co-opetition, already mentioned, will be emphasized repeatedly: the fulcrum is rarely set at the center point between cooperation and competition. Finding the synthesis point or sweet spot is not about "balance" in the sense of perfect equilibrium; successful fulcrum points prove to be where "asymmetric balance" is achieved—like the asymmetric balance of an outrigger canoe driven by the wind (see the cover of this book). And as this work will show, the more successful operations generally give greater weight to the competition side of the scale—metaphorically, in the main hull of the outrigger as distinguished from in the outrigged pontoon.

By whose rules is the proper mix defined and identified?

Much of this work is devoted to answering that question. But just knowing and understanding that finding a synthesis of cooperation and competition should be kept foremost in our minds when analyzing problems; it will take us most of the way there— most of the way to the sweet spot. In that way, we more clearly can analyze our issues and promulgate our laws and rules, whether great or small, for the individual or for the collective, or for both together.

But when do we know when we are all the way there, i.e. when have we achieved the ultimate synthesis? It is when we have sensed the sweet spot for the particular solution in question, or for life, or for existence, or for the asymmetric balance. It is when we've found the "zone." You'll know it when the business hums, when the music swings, when the system gels, when society thrives to her maximum effectiveness, when all parts synergize.

2

Definitions
and Explanations

WHAT TO EXPECT

Soon we shall test this theory of co-opetition. The concept is found in, and proof of it is offered from, the fields of anthropology, biophysics, and philosophy, and clarified with examples from art, music, and other fields. We will demonstrate that natural points of synthesis, once positioned, can enable those on opposite political, economic, or social poles to find common ground on which to coexist peacefully and beneficially.

Please be mindful that I will often alternatively use the term "the synthesis" or "synthesis" to mean the same as "co-opetition." Note that from the perspective of co-opetition, "coexisting" does not mean merely "compromising." As previously mentioned, it does not suggest perfect balance or harmony, like a lever weighted equally at opposing extremes. Co-opetition theory, as noted above, implies an asymmetric balance—a point where blending, unification, fusion, merger, mixture, and amalgamation occur.

To "synthesize" means to combine parts into a single component or entity. But how does one find the point where synthesis occurs? I will explain this fully in coming chapters.

It bears emphasizing here, though, that co-opetition, or the synthesis, is a paradigm intended to assist us in reaching optimum functionality in our endeavors, whether in personal relationships, understanding ourselves and the world, or seeking ways to better govern ourselves. In that last regard, for example, we have confirmation that the Founding Fathers of the United States of America got it right: The U.S. Constitution is the greatest political charter ever written. I'll show why.

To re-emphasize: merely recognizing that the points of synthesis exist in all of nature, and being willing to find those points in given situations, will bring people nearer one another in understanding. My hope and belief is that it will also bring governments with countervailing interests closer to reconciling with one another. The last chapter of my novel The Tortoise Shell Game demonstrates this theme.

Up to now in our history the human race has achieved some successes in this endeavor; for even war, arguably the most competitive system on earth, resulted in the development of the humanitarian rules of the Geneva Convention. Under the theory espoused here, though, we will learn to achieve syntheses more quickly and at far lower cost.

The co-opetition concept relates to the entire spectrum of human culture. It can assist us in evaluating different political, economic, social, legal, and environmental points of view, and provide a basis for the analysis of many of the problems facing the world today.

DEFINITIONS

Proper communication is a highly cooperative matter, so as we proceed it's crucial that we use the same terms with the same understanding of their meaning. In this work, I use certain words in a specialized manner; here are the most critical definitions and the ways in which the terms interact.

Competition is defined for our purposes as: the conduct of any individual, entity, group, or nation that takes a benefit for him/itself from other individuals, nations, life forms, or even the environment. Said differently, something is "competitionistic" (slightly different from competitive) if it evinces a tendency to:

- take or separate
- break apart
- disunite
- cause chaos
- become individualistic

Looked at another way, something is competitionistic if it resists bonding or association—if it is dominated by self-interest.

EXAMPLES OF COMPETITION

A few examples of competition include the constant quest for food, mates, shelter, and security (the basic elements of natural selection and the survival of the fittest); the urge for freedom, self-protection, and the expression of self-rights; reproductive and sexual pursuits; ambition; hate; jealousy; anger; crime; avoidance of taxation; warfare; sports; and many others.

My novel *The Tortoise Shell Game* captures a scene one dark night when Egan James blind-sides Anthony Darren. Blood, wrath, and raw emotion erupt in the alley where onlookers circled—ultimate competition.

Cooperation, on the other hand, is defined here as: any conduct of an individual, entity, group, or nation that tries to benefit, or thinks it is benefiting, other individuals, entities, groups, nations, other forms of life, or the environment. Conduct that fits our definition usually occurs for group or mutual-welfare considerations. Something is "cooperationistic" (slightly different from cooperative) if it tends to:

- unite
- bind, bond
- attract
- become orderly or collective
- force together—e.g. involuntary, compulsory cooperation

Something is cooperationistic when it draws together other individuals, entities, groups, or nations, or even things.

Therefore, "competition" as defined in this work includes the elements of taking and separating, whereas "cooperation" has within it the elements of giving and uniting, bestowing benevolence, and forcing cooperation.

EXAMPLES OF COOPERATION

It's easy to find examples of cooperation: the urge of humans to protect and aid the group to which they belong, their fellow man, and their families; to follow leaders; to bond, love, and feel sympathy, empathy, and compassion; to be benevolent; to smile;

to have esprit de corps; to drop money into the red kettle at Christmas time.

In *The Tortoise Shell Game,* we see Anthony and his friends swimming in giant surf off La Jolla, California. They discover they are caught in a rip tide as they try to reach shore. His muscles locked in exhaustion, Anthony hears Joe's call for help. Without thinking twice Anthony goes to Joe's aid—almost losing his own life.

However, cooperation also may be an involuntary act. For example, in submitting to laws, to regulation, or paying taxes. Most people drive at or near the speed limit because they choose to; others, only because they have to. A dictator imposing his will on the people is a form of "involuntary cooperation"; a police state would be the ultimate example of forced cooperation.

Cooperation can also occur through naiveté, ambivalence, stupidity, and lack of due diligence or through bribery, corruption, or just plain negligence. Also, cooperation can be given in payment for something that is expected in return—such as food, money or safety.

I alluded to chaos when I described the various aspects of competition—but what does competition have to do with chaos? And what does cooperation have to do with order? How are these equations reconciled?

Remember that cooperation and competition are not by any means limited to human life. Although we will go into the subject in detail in later chapters, for now remember that we are all made of stardust. When subatomic particles work together in waves and patterns—that is, in cooperation—they are in unity. This occurs, for example, when gravity combines particles (causing accretion—a form of forced cooperation), as when making a planet. (Let's pause a bit. There is a lighter side to the weight of all this gravity: Jay Leno once asked people on the street why the moon orbits the earth. An auto mechanic replied: "To get to the other side." Now back to the theme.) On the other hand, when molecules or particles explode, fight with, or repel one another, they are in a state of chaos, which by our definition places them in competition against one another for space.

Co-opetition, *aka the synthesis, or ultimate synthesis,* then, refers to finding what the philosopher Friedrich Hegel would call, a "synthesis of the opposites," I add here a synthesis between the opposites of cooperation and competition. As I've said, I will also use the euphemisms: "synthesis, Mother Nature's magic," or finding the "sweet spot," or sometimes, "Adam Smith's Invisible Hand," as expressing the same meaning as the synthesis of co-opetition.

Again, co-opetition does not mean the point of perfect balance or homeostasis between cooperation and competition. Balance equals motionlessness, equilibrium, steadiness; that is, lack of change. But in nature, any system in perfect balance does not endure for long; change is inevitable, if only in the form of entropy. Therefore wisdom dictates making sure that, whenever possible, change flows in a desirable direction.

In human terms, we call this guided flow progress—and as we shall see, the engine that drives progress is predominantly competition but includes cooperation. And, that's the reason for the general rule that the optimum point of asymmetric balance between cooperation and competition must usually be placed toward the side of competition . However, there are exceptions, as we shall see.

Again, what we're seeking to achieve is what I call Ultimate Synthesis. Laws and social mores, although consciously conceived, are ultimately the involuntary products of human beings trying to synthesize their instinctive impulses toward competition and cooperation. The very urge to survive contains these two bundles of traits. They are woven into our cells—in the form of co-opetition. As I will show, examples abound. For now, I will demonstrate only a few of them, so you get the picture before we get too far ahead of ourselves.

WINE-MAKING AND A FEW OTHER EXAMPLES

The hands-on method of getting a little help from nature to achieve synthesis is like making a fine bottle of wine. Keep in mind as you read this part that order, as I use the term here, should be regarded as a form of cooperation, whereas chaos in this discussion should be regarded as a form of competition. Generally speaking, elements that come together tend to become orderly, they cooperate with each other. On the other hand, elements that separate or break apart tend to become chaotic—that is, they compete with each other.

For years, I grew vines and made wine, a family tradition. You start by picking grapes that are ripe—that is, they are in a perfect state of cooperation with nature—order prevails. Then you violently crush and de-stem them and set them roiling in a fermentation vat—chaos prevails. You've just commenced competing with nature.

The sugar in the juice, catalyzed by the yeast naturally found on the grape skins—or perhaps store-bought yeast—begins to convert to alcohol. The elements are becoming orderly—they are becoming cooperative while transforming.

Several days later, at the time the best synthesis of co-opetition is reached (or you could say, when the sweet spot is found), the roiling ends and you transfer this green young wine into barrels. You are now getting cooperation—forced cooperation—out of the elements of your wine. The wine matures in the barrels for a year or two or even longer—more forced cooperation—until it reaches another point of synthesis and it's time for bottling.

Meanwhile you've "racked" the wine a few times, i.e. cleaned out the dead yeast and debris that collects in the bottom of the barrels—more cooperation.

Eventually, at the optimum time for a new synthesis, you bottle the wine. But this is still not the highest and best state of synthesis for drinking the wine. That is determined by the type of wine you've made—red, white, heavy or light—each will have a different point of optimum taste or its own point of ultimate synthesis, its sweet spot, its best point of coopetition.

Now, if you don't watch it, if you allow the wine to age too long in the bottle, entropy (chaos) will set in. The chemicals comprising the wine will break down at too great a rate. Perhaps oxygen atoms that sneaked in during processing excessively oxidize the wine: a form of competition between the elements of this heretofore beautiful synthesis you've created. Over-competition—too much chaos—has now ruined your wine.

Other illustrations of ultimate synthesis are easily found. For instance, in bicycle racing or motor racing the riders or drivers often "draft" off each other: they ride in the slipstream of air that the forward vehicle creates for them. Sometimes racers work in teams, cooperating by changing places with one another to break through the air even as they compete with one another to win the race: co-opetition. However, when the drafting is not cooperatively done, it is straight competition.

Or consider the example of a couple of business competitors: let's call them Pacific Motors and Atlantic Motors. They jointly (cooperatively) develop a new engine for their cars, yet continue to compete to sell their separate cars in the marketplace. That's coopetition.

Then there is the example of the National Football League: The member teams cooperate by sharing TV revenues in order to help level the financial playing field and make the games more interesting—yet on the real playing field, they fight it out in full-on competition.

You will find another example of reaching the synthesis in Daniel James Brown's 2014 book, *The Boys in a Boat*. It's about how the 8-man U.S. rowing team won the gold medal in the 1936 Olympics in Berlin, Germany. Leading up to the games, the coach of the University of Washington's team couldn't figure out why his individually great rowers could not gel or find their sweet spot as a team. He believed that reaching such a level was essential for getting them to their optimum speeds. Their timing and synchronization seemed perfect, yet the boat didn't "swing." The competition part of the effort was impeccable; but how about the cooperation side?

The coach explained that to get the boat to "swing" they should row as a band of brothers; they should love each other as teammates. They apparently got the point because they began feeling a greater cooperative bond among them. T hey gelled. The boat began to "swing." They got into the "zone." They won with the fastest time for that event in Olympic history.

3

Codification of the Rule

SYNTHESIZING CO-OPETITION

As I've said before, at first the forces of competition and cooperation seem opposite and irreconcilable. But, in fact, the universe requires that they be synthesized for life to exist at all. The traits of cooperation and competition are each composed of a bundle of sub-traits. The elements that make up each bundle are, themselves, constantly changing and shifting, striving always to remain in synthesis.

In music, for example, basic harmony generally falls far into the cooperation arena. But dissonance, which can be found in a multitude of beautiful chords, brings competition into the synthesis.

Or take leadership: to command and direct others often involves competing to gain or remain in power. Yet, at the same time, leading or commanding others for their benefit is a form of cooperating with them.

The word, discipline, if administered justly and reasonably, may in many cases also be regarded as a form of synthesis, or coopetition. This is because the act of voluntarily acquiescence to discipline is a form of cooperation, while at the same time, the one who imposes discipline on others competes—engages in a form of competition—with them. Thus, the act of administering discipline to instruct and help those being disciplined—as in parenting, school, sports, or the military—is a cooperative function. This good form of discipline, this competitive cooperation, exemplifies co-opetition.

It's important to emphasize that although nature—or God— seems to strive for harmony, true harmony in nature (or in God's nature) generally is not represented by perfect balance. For growth and development to exist, there must be some imbalance or asymmetry, in the synthesis.

As philosopher Frederich Hegel put it, "Strife is growth." Not too much strife, mind you, just enough to promote growth. Sadly, some philosophers and revolutionaries, such as Karl Marx and Joseph Stalin, took Hegel's comment to mean that "the ends justify the means"—even to the extent of sanctioning or ordering mass killings of those who did not cooperate.

This illustrates that in human life, factors associated with high levels of consciousness constantly interfere with attaining or maintaining optimum synthesis. Oftentimes, man seeks to actively correct what he perceives to be an imbalance, unfairness, or wrong. If not armed with knowledge of how both the competing and cooperating factors play a role in such situations, we can make mistakes and act in ways that, like King Musa sowing too much gold throughout North Africa, will result in unintended negative consequences.

THE MOBILE

Imagine a giant mobile of great complexity hanging from the sky. Touch any piece of it, and other, unexpected pieces shift in unpredictable directions, possibly with undesired results. The lesson is that if you don't consider the possible consequences of what you intend to do, synthesis will often not be achieved. On a large scale, however, the aggregate of individuals that compose the human race strive for co-opetition continuously, either intentionally or unconsciously, and in their own individual ways. Therefore, the natural fulcrum of the co-opetition synthesis is whatever point provides the greatest survivability and quality of life for the species, its individuals, and its genes.

But keep the mobile analogy in mind. An axiomatic consequence of moving a tipping point is the realization that its optimum position must also achieve the conservation of substantially all other life and resources, including the earth itself. Yet "conservation" should not result in the extinction, impoverishment, or de-evolution of mankind.

Optimizing the synthesis to reach the highest level of operation of a system is the key to true co-opetition—the Primal Wisdom of nature.

For Co-opetition in Triangulation or Realms. See Endnotes.

How Miscellaneous Words Relate To Co-opetition		
Words below related to:	Words below related to:	Words below related to:
Cooperation	The Synthesis	Competition
=	=	=
Order	Sweet Spot	Chaos
Love	v	Hate
Gravity (the force)	v	Electromagnetism
Quiescence	v	Big Bang
Contraction	v	Expansion
Collectivism	v	Individualism
Totalitarianism	v	Liberty
Smile	v	Frown
Censorship	v	Free Speech
Consonance	Harmony	Dissonance
Taxes	v	Tax-Free
Dormant	v	Growth
Big Government	v	Limited Government
Socialism	capitalism (business)	Free Market
Positive: e.g. Mentoring	Leadership	Negative: e.g. Discipline
Altruism	v	Egoism
Acquiescence	v	Resistance

4

Biophysical Inquiry

CO-OPETITION IS NATURAL

In the universe, forces exist that bring things together and that cause them to coalesce or combine. Gravity, which draws all particles of matter toward one another, is a prime example of this. On the opposite side of the equation is the electromagnetic force, which, together with subatomic radiation and decay, act to separate, degrade, break down and repel particles. This array is evidenced by decaying particles and heat radiation, the "big bang" phenomena, the dispersal of energy, entropy, and many other physical actions and events.

Thus, every particle of matter generally is composed of dual forces: those that are competitive and those that are cooperative. The extreme of competitiveness results in chaos. The extreme of cooperativeness results in excessive order, or stagnation. The cooperative forces combine, coalesce, or gather in wave forms.

Competitive forces separate, repel, or act randomly. Because all forms of life, including human beings, are composed of materials manufactured by the stars, perhaps we received our behavioral traits from the very competitive/cooperative physical particles that make up our bodies.

This is one reason I propose that human nature tends toward co-opetition—because the universe itself is co-opetitive. This idea is not outlandish. I re-emphasize: in the universe, forces cause particles to either repel each other and fight for space or they coalesce matter or collect particles in waves. These forces often cause oscillation through a temporary balanced state, which is a condition close to co-opetition.

Manifestations of co-opetition in the physical world include chemical crystals, snowflakes, spiral galaxies, tree leaves, spider webs, and computer-generated spontaneous fractals. They also include multicellular animals whose cells in primordial times lived separately, like bees in the hive, but which, through evolution, came to cooperate and combine for their mutual survival and replication.

We are amazed by the combined order and chaos of the double helix of DNA or the synthesis of cooperation and competition in the design of the chambered nautilus shell. Notice that the shell is not precisely machined: there is some chaos in that order. Nothing in nature is precisely machined; there is some chaos in all the order found in nature. This demonstrates that there is co-opetition in nature.

As a general rule, if you go against nature you are going in the wrong direction. Every eighth atomic weight has properties similar to eight weights up or down. In music, every eighth note up the scale is the same, being an octave higher or lower. These are examples of order—a form of cooperation.

The solar systems and galaxies of our universe, with their planets and stars held together by gravity while simultaneously attempting to fly off in all directions, represent a form of loose equilibrium between the competitive and cooperative physical forces. At the same time, each system oscillates to the influence of the opposing forces.

Similarly, the atmosphere and the surface environment of the earth exemplify a very delicate balance: the carbon dioxide released by animal life and the oxygen released by plant life working together in a non-conscious, co-opetitive balance—a balance that keeps both kingdoms of organisms alive.

In such examples, we find an irrefutable correlation of physics to organic life and from there to human behavior, even to the demand for human rights. Maintaining strong rights for individuals (competitive rights) and the group (cooperative rights) is essential to attaining optimum synthesis in the lives of social creatures such as human beings.

THE UNBALANCED UNIVERSE

Entropy is the measure of perpetually increasing decay and chaos. The second law of thermodynamics declares that in any closed system in the universe, entropy (chaos/ competition) always increases, while order (cooperation) always decreases. Bicycles rust, food decays, animals grow old, and batteries wear out: all examples of entropy. However, this leads to a prime question: if the universe is a place that constantly winds down like a clock, how did it come together in the first place?

How did life, that most elegant example of the synthesis of competition and cooperation, not only begin but evolve into ever more complicated forms, in clear defiance of the second law of thermodynamics? The explanation lies in the cooperative forces in nature—and for believers, I do not exclude the hand of God. To re-emphasize: entropy is evidence of competition between particles, while order is evidence of cooperation between particles. Thus matter is a manifestation of the forces of cooperation, whereas energy dispersal and entropy reveal the forces of competition.

Forces generating cooperation and order fight entropy—but if too much order is generated, movement ceases, matter freezes, and growth is stymied. Thus, finding the right synthesis—the right point of co-opetition—is the goal for enabling growth. Within the atomic nucleus itself, the "three forces"—electromagnetism and the strong and weak nuclear forces—interact by moving subatomic particles to various states or sometimes to complete annihilation.

Increased energy in the system means greater competition amongst particles—which, if the competition grows too great, could lead to total chaos—to explosion. On the other hand, the less energy used by the system, the greater the cooperation and order in that system—up to the point that change and growth end. Under these circumstances, heat would give way to such cold temperatures that particles could no longer move to different states. The result? Stagnation. Death.

Astrophysicists do not know the ultimate fate of the universe as a whole. It is on the borderline between collapsing (cooperation) and expanding (competition). Most experts now insist that it will expand forever, degrading into individual particles that never interact. However, others predict that entirely new universes will bubble out of the material of this one, or that the universe will oscillate from one big bang to another for all eternity.

In the grand scheme of the principle of co-opetition, there are entities within realms that compete and cooperate with each other. As noted above, when three or more groups or individuals compete for the same goal, the issues of realms often arise. I earlier referenced this nuance in the Appendix as "triangulation." However, as we will see, nature seeks to achieve co-opetition within each realm and even between realms. For example, the semblance of order in the universe would be an "outer" realm, while the ecological balance of a pond in the woods would be more of an "inner" realm.

Thus, governing loops (to be explained later in detail in the Anthropology section) within a realm often keep exponential growth in check. It often happens by multi-realm competition; the result is a tendency toward maintaining a synthesized steady state of co-opetition throughout all realms. They are interconnected.

Regarding the entire realm of the earth itself, such is reminiscent of the Gaia Hypothesis advocated by James Lovelock and co-developed by Lynn Margoles during the period from the 1970s to the 1990s. They regarded mother earth and her environment as a self-regulating organism.

RELATIONSHIP TO ORDER AND CHAOS

In a nutshell: we realize that in nature almost every chaotic thing—such as a storm or turbulence in a river flow—has lurking within the chaos a pattern of orderliness. Examples abound: the events of chaos showing up in computer fractal models that then develop orderly patterns; or the bizarre randomness of one hundred foot-high killer waves that appear to arise suddenly in the vast oceans. In order for this to happen, the right conditions must exist. Research indicates that such monster waves sometimes result from smaller waves randomly combining to form an increasing resonance. Resonance also explains why, in 1940, a suspension bridge in Tacoma, Washington started to oscillate like a snake until it collapsed in a windstorm it was supposedly designed to handle.

How does this relate to the theory of co-opetition? Chaos is a form of competition, and order a form of cooperation. In nature, we find an ongoing oscillation between chaos and order, with a synthesis forming during the transition event. I believe that nature moving toward this state of synthesis is what produces growth. Fortunately for us, it's also the state best suited for generating life.

So, what is the normal state of the universe? Could it not comprise of the everlasting, continuing process of the instant creation and annihilation of particles and antiparticles? Under that condition nothing would exist—no stars, no planets, no matter. Nothing tangible or discernable would be evident. If so, such state obviously did not exist forever? A triggering event occurred. There are now stars and planets out there.

So, did a random event cause the universe to fall temporarily out of balance? Did such a random event trigger the explosion of the universe into existence—as depicted by Ted Packman's background of the cover of this book. Could it be that such event of turbulence triggered the Big Bang itself? And that such a disturbance generated an asymmetry in the universe—namely more particles in relation to antiparticles? If so, could this imbalance have ignited the Big Bang and created a growing disparity that the universe has been trying to restore to symmetry ever since? Is it that those "interruption events," such as the Big Bang, continue and randomly recur again and again over time?

If so, the universe could be in the process of passing through a hundred billion years or more of existence while in the course of correcting that initial disturbance. Let's find out whether the ratio of particles to antiparticles is moving toward symmetry or equilibrium or away from it—while recognizing, again, that the process has a long way to go. Most particle physicists believe that at the moment of the Big Bang, particles and antimatter particles were in symmetry with one another—but soon slid away from this symmetry. However, at this writing, nobody can explain why this happened (see *The Mystery of the Missing Antimatter*, Helen R. Quinn and Yossi Nir, 2008). At the end of the hypothetical corrective process, will the universe be relegated to this theoretical normal state of, as I call it, quiescence—no stars, no time, and no existence as we know it? The universe would then consist of nothing but particles and anti-particles, now back in symmetry, annihilating one another. Did God create quiescence and then ignite the Big Bang?

(See Appendix, infra, for further notes on this subject of Unbalanced Universe)

ROLE OF NATURAL SELECTION

Of course, we all recognize and emphasize that natural selection played a major role in the development of cooperation in life and among species. It facilitated a natural tendency. In the typical model, cooperation behavior helped the particular form of life in question to survive and replicate. ("Why We Help: The Evolution of Cooperation," Martin A. Nowak, *Scientific American*, June 19, 2012.) As an aside, noted science philosopher/ evolutionary biologist, Stephen C. Meyer, Ph.D., proffers in his book *Darwin's Doubt* (2013) that life must have had an intelligent source. He cites the unexplained complication and order of the designs of the Cambrian explosion to complex life with no fossil record evident of the transition to it; thus it must have come from an intelligent source. I believe it is a result of nature's co-opetition at work; but such belief does not close the door on Meyer's theory that intelligence played a role in these designs, or, I add, a role in co-opetition itself.

One final point on biophysics, Shewanella: Dr. Kenneth Nelson of the University of Southern California, wonders whether we will find this mind-blowing species of bacteria on Mars. (See "Have we found Alien life?", Corey S. Powell, *Popular Mechanics,* 2015).This possible extra-terrestrial bacteria eats electricity. They call it the Shewanella bacteria, detected by plunging electros into the biosphere, soil, rocks, etc. Nelson says: "Their earth seems to be a world built on cooperation a far cry from the more familiar one of cutthroat [Darwinian] competition." I predict that eventually they will, nevertheless, find co-opetition in its make-up, but this time with the emphasis on cooperation rather than from competition

5

What Did the Philosophers Say?

Human beings might be the stuff of stars, but along the way we acquired a remarkably advanced, if not unique, form of thinking we call "consciousness." As social animals, we devote considerable amounts of this power to dealing with one another. Over time, this has resulted in various sets of rules and directives about how to get along that we call "morals." Justifying, explaining, and rationalizing morality is the job of philosophers.

What, if anything, have philosophers had to say about co-opetition in the human sphere?

They never used that word, of course, but most of the great Western philosophers, beginning with Socrates, spoke of the struggle between egoism (selfishness/ competition) and altruism (benevolence/cooperation). As said earlier, I propose that co-opetition is a synthesis of these two traits, and as such, the ideal and natural state of man is when he enters the intuitive quest for such synthesis.

When Rousseau spoke of the Native American tribesman as the "noble savage," I interpret "noble" as cooperative, and "savage" as competitive. Among many other examples, I also include the yin/yang dichotomy of Taoist Eastern philosophy, which refers to the necessary balance of opposing parts leading to a harmonious whole.

Even as recently as 1993, Dee Hock, the founder and former CEO of the VISA credit card association, coined the word "chaordic" in a speech given to the Santa Fe Institute. The word is a portmanteau referring to a system of organization that blends characteristics of chaos and order. I had been circulating manuscripts of co-opetition theory in the late 1980s, wherein I associated order with cooperation and associated chaos to extreme competition. It's too bad Dee Hock and I were not aware of each other at the time. We would have had much to share.

Also, pursuing a parallel track in mathematics, economics and business Game Theory, John Forbes Nash, winner of a 1994 Nobel Prize, spoke of "Equilibrium" as a word to describe a synthesis of competition and cooperation. We recall how wonderfully actor Russell Crowe played Nash in the movie, *A Beautiful Mind*. Among other books, in 2007, Harold Kuhn and Sylvia Nasar described Nash's theories in *The Essential John Nash*, Princeton University Press. Scholars refer to his Nash Equilibrium as synonymous with coopetition in its truest sense. I had written of what I called co-opetition as a theory to be applied universally, including in political science, economics, and social science. Some years later, I was happy to learn that Nash had independently begun applying essentially the same concept to Game Theory in business and economics.

The principle of co-opetition asserts that an important characteristic of humankind's nature is the urge to balance in some way—often asymmetrically—the apparently opposing bundles of competitive and cooperative drives. We can find this idea reflected implicitly over and over again in the words of the philosophers.

For those who seriously study philosophy, please allow me to speak to you briefly. This co-opetitive concept is consistent with Kant's mediation of Hobbesian egoism (competition) weighed with Lockeian considerations of morality (cooperation). Neither Hobbes ("man is competitive to a fault") nor Locke ("man reasons and cooperates") appeared to clearly argue that nature is itself constantly striving for a synthesis of the two traits and that both are necessary. Instead, to these philosophers, the synthesis occurs through the social contract by which man gives up some of his egoistic competitiveness in exchange for some collective or altruistic action and the protection of the group.

G. W. Friedrich Hegel, on the other hand, argued that human rights are "inalienable" and should never be given up. (In my view, this means man should continue competing for such rights.) He argued that mankind is endowed with individual rights, but that obedience (cooperation) is also required. The problem with the modern world, he asserted, is its failure to construct a social and political order that satisfies the claims of both individuals and the collective.

I define "the claims of both" as the urge to synthesize the individual drive for human rights (egoism-competitive) with the demands for group (social-cooperative) benefit. The best synthesis lies somewhere between these two drives, or is a synthesis thereof, and achieves co-opetition through integrating what later philosophers labeled "thesis and antithesis." In Hegel's view, through this dialectic process, a synthesis that leads to truth will be found. Unfortunately as was mentioned before, some followers of Karl Marx twisted the idea of "antithesis" into justification to break entirely with the status quo, and also, that the ends often justify the means. However, a thesis with no antithesis equals unbridled cooperation—and cooperation with no antithesis has no counterbalance.

Perhaps Hegel was never clearly understood, or perhaps many of his divided disciples simply did not realize that in actuality he was talking about what we now refer to as co-opetition. In my interpretation of his words, Hegel was saying—that the ultimate purpose of human attainment is to properly synthesize the demands of individuals with the demands of societies.

Overburdening one aspect against the other is detrimental to any governmental or social system. Overburdening the cooperation side—which includes forced cooperation—can lead, for example, to the stagnation of the economy. On the other hand, overburdening the competition side can lead to anarchy or great crime, including devastating business crime—witness the financial debacle of Bernie Madoff's colossal Ponzi scheme.

Hegel argued that in government, the State is the formal instrument of reason, which he divides into parts representing the "forces" of the "particularity" (individuality/competitiveness) and "universality" (collectivism/cooperation). The structure of the State, he believed, should be carefully designed so as to balance the influence of these forces.

As we shall see, this principle is well-represented in the American Constitution, whose function is to mediate the naturally occurring tension between man's competitive and cooperative traits, including both competition between states and the federal government and cooperation (forced or voluntary) with the federal government.

THE HIDDEN ("INVISIBLE") HAND

Moralist/philosopher/economist Adam Smith asserted in his works *The Theory of Moral Sentiments,* and *An Inquiry into the Nature and Causes of the Wealth of Nations,* that self-interest plays a natural and beneficial role in a free enterprise (capitalist) system. But he perceived that a moral hook on that role of self-interest existed—a hook much overlooked by just about everyone—including most liberals and some conservatives alike.

In a true free enterprise system, he said, individuals would naturally tend to rise above strictly selfish interests to the level of mutual benefit or benevolent self-interest. Thus, even back in the late 1700s Adam Smith was talking about capitalism as benefiting from what I call the "co-opetitive" traits of humankind.

I emphasize that there is an intuitive cooperative aspect to the otherwise wholly competitive nature of capitalism—and again, co-opetition most often works because it is natural. This natural human tendency for benevolent self-interest in the operation of capitalism is a form of intuition, according to Dr. Roger Frantz and Dr. Alex Pattakos in their book *Intuition at Work.* It stands to reason that… If you can't trust the person you would do business with, you will not likely do business with him. Ethics and morality are integral to a good business relationship. Thus, cooperation is much of what makes Adam Smith's invisible hand work.

In the late 1800s, Friedrich Nietzsche argued that the dominant force of history is the "will to power," and to mitigate this there should be a "trans valuation of values" wherein the "feminine" virtues (e. g. compassion, empathy, sensitivity etc.—forms of cooperation) would merge with the "masculine" virtues (e. g. strength, aggressiveness, impassion etc.—forms of competition), to achieve greatness rather than mere goodness.

Other philosophers, using different terminology, also wrote about the importance of balancing competing and cooperating forces. John Stuart Mill (the father), among others, is noted for his ideas on synthesizing the prominence of individual rights over group interests. He said: "A society that will trade a little liberty for a little order will lose both, and deserve neither." He is further quoted as saying: "The only freedom which deserves the name is that of pursuing our own good in our own way, so long as we do not attempt to deprive others of theirs, or impede their efforts to obtain it. Each is the proper guardian of his own health, whether bodily, or mentally, or spiritually. Mankind are greater gainers by suffering each other to live as seems good to themselves, than by compelling each to live as seems good to the rest."

How do these ideas conform to what we know about the workings of society in the real world? I contend that it is the distortion of the innate urge to synthesize our egoistic/altruistic natures that gets humankind into trouble.

Specifically, I do not believe that humans in general have to be trained to be unselfish (although certainly a few do); we find that as people mature, they learn how to gauge how much of each commodity they and their loved ones need to survive or even thrive. As they gain experience, people also gain their "essence," as existentialist Jean Paul Sartre would say. Attempting to shift responsibility for this choice from the individual to the collective is—as I believe John Stuart Mill would agree—an example of overloading the synthesis in the direction of cooperation. In this regard, it seems obvious that political conservatives generally believe more in self-help and less in governmental aid than do liberals; thus, they are more likely to individually cooperate with and privately contribute to others. In fact, according to a story aired in 2006 on ABC's 20/20, the more politically and fiscally conservative a person is, the more likely that he will contribute to charity.

Furthermore, relative wealth is not the largest factor in determining who gives and how much. This reflects the fact that liberals generally believe more in cooperation as manifested by the government, and therefore, have expectations that the government will or should supply the "charity"; conservatives, on the other hand, shift the synthesis more toward the competition side and thus, according to the 20/20 story, generally feel they are personally responsible for assisting their fellow human beings.

By the way, revealing their prowess at the art of public relations, someone on the left side of the political spectrum, I am sure, also commandeered the color blue from the Republican Party. I guess democrats did not like red, their previous color. After all, red is the color of communism. (AlterNet and the Washington Post, according to Wikipedia, said it first happened on the Today show on October 30, 2000.) Before then, the mascot elephant of the Republicans always was depicted as blue, and the Republican states were shown as blue states. On the contrary, the donkey, the mascot of the Democrats, was always depicted as red, and the Democrat states were red.

When one or more of the national television networks reversed the colors, the Republicans were apparently sleeping at the switch and did nothing about it. Or perhaps they considered a color change as irrelevant. The former blue Republican states are now the red states. Conservative old timers, I understand, still have a hard time getting used to that reversal.

6

Anthropological and Historical Inquiry

GOVERNING LOOPS

The great anthropologist Gregory Bateson studied biological and evolving systems (e.g., insect colonies, animal herds). In *Steps to an Ecology of Mind,* he said that such systems consist of elements that are potentially regenerative; that they will go into exponential "runaway" growth if uncorrected by outside forces. In our analysis, such unrestrained growth represents an extreme form of competition.

Fortunately, in nature, such conditions rarely occur for long; biological systems are generally kept at near a steady state by governing loops, including disease and predation. In my view, such loops are forms of "non-conscious cooperation;" At times the cooperation may be voluntary, or it may be forced or induced.

It is a means to control both runaway growth and exponential competition. I call it "non-conscious" because cooperation of this sort is not decided upon, but is an intrinsic aspect of life and nature. Take for example of the relationship of the wolf to herds of animals—such as caribou or deer. Predators prey on the week and the unfit first. They thereby cull the weaker genes from the gene-pool of the caribou. This strengthens the eventual survivability of the herd. The beneficial side-effect of the predation is the wolf's indirect cooperation for the survival of the herd.

Runaway growth of any particular form of life will generally not endure to the detriment of all other forms of life. Generally, nature non-consciously (or God-consciously) decides what forms of growth should continue, or are desirable, and what forms should be cut back or governed. The matter can also be looked at another way: Something causes competition to arise in order to cut back exponential growth. The fact that new competition comes to the rescue means that something is non-consciously cooperating with the overall system to keep it in a state of repair and sustainability.

Who or what makes these decisions, if anyone, is beyond any human's capacity to answer—except perhaps for those with faith in God or in the non-conscious (instinctive, automatic) workings of an intelligence in nature.

Still, sixty-five million years ago it took a giant meteor to impose a governing loop upon the exponential growth of the dinosaur. Such an intervention was obviously not caused by the workings of earthly nature.

In other words, the freedom to do anything one may wish (competition) will be automatically or non-consciously governed and restrained (forced cooperation) for the benefit of the system. Those individuals who choose to conform to and acquiesce in restraint can be said to cooperate. The legal implications of this are obvious: the development of law and regulation is a form of such restraint, voluntary or otherwise, and forced cooperation.

In the grand realm of nature, governing loops are the work of factors that non-consciously "cooperate" to outbalance and control runaway activity or growth. By chance or by design, this benefits environmental and ecological systems, including the life forms within them.

For the Tukano Indians of the Amazon basin, human actions are regulated in a way that curtails long-term harmful effects to the environment (cooperation), while still allowing the group to extract material products (competition with the environment) for survival and social satisfaction. They protect the forest margins along the Orinoco and upper Amazon River from deforestation, thus allowing the fisheries to gorge and replenish themselves when the annual floods come. Rather than relying upon conscious and specific laws, the Tukano and most other native people in the Amazon invoke a pervasive system of moral injunctions based on a form of group spiritual understanding. Admittedly, at times the approach used by some native peoples to maintain such systems can be, and has been violent and oppressive—but they typically work.

In Chapter 13, Synthesizing Conservative and Liberal Extremes, I will discuss: *Guns, Germs and Steel,* and *Collapse,* by noted anthropologist Jared M. Diamond. Ph.D. His works discuss prehistoric societies and why some of them collapsed. I wanted the reader to first gain the perspective of discussions on political and economic systems before applying Diamond's work to coopetition. That is why I discuss his works later, in the political chapters.

Early 20th century political philosopher/anarchist Peter Kropotkin was among the first to specifically propose the idea that mutual benefit plays just as large a role in evolution as does mutual strife; i.e., the strife found in Darwin's survival of the fittest. (I disagree, however, with his general philosophy on Anarchy.) William Sumner called this same process of the mutual benefit/mutual strife equation as: "antagonistic cooperation."

Similarly, Alexis De Tocqueville's observations of American democracy in the early nineteenth century are interspersed with comments about the competitive/cooperative characteristics of an evolving democratic system.

A review of aspects of trench warfare during World War I demonstrates the co-opetition theory at work. The troops on opposite sides developed an unspoken code of ethics, a form of cooperation. In certain situations, they could walk around in full view outside their trenches without firing upon one another—an unspoken temporary cease fire. But then, on silent schedule, these interludes would conclude and the war revives between them.

7

Cultural Examples

If this theory of co-opetition is truly universal, it must apply in all fields, even cultural ones. Let's see if it does.

MUSIC

Is music necessary for survival? Why did the human species invent or discover music in the first place? We know that human beings are great modifiers of their environment. In an early scene in *The Tortoise Shell Game*, Anthony observes a mother and her child on the beach north of La Jolla. He is struck with a question as he sees the child begin drawing circles and building sand castles almost immediately upon being set loose. Was the child competing with nature? Or was he trying to cooperate and bring some order to it?

It is logical, therefore, to assume that our ancestors took noise, segregated it into individual sounds, recombined them

with ordered timing, and thus, invented music. They were mod-
ifying the sounds of nature around them. The question is, did
they do this in a subconscious effort to create melody and rhythm
by injecting order (cooperation) into chaotic noise or discord
(competition)?

We observe that the act of competing when balanced with
cooperation creates harmony. To compete without cooperating
results in discordance. In music, a harmonious (cooperative)
chord that contains a spice of dissonance (competition) can be
very beautiful.

For example, an A minor 7th chord (A,C,E,G) features dissonance between the G and A when those two notes alone are
played together; but adding the E and C creates a harmonious
chord. A co-opetition synthesis occurs.

I queried musicologist/classical arranger Donald Balestrieri
on this subject. First, he enthusiastically endorsed the idea of
metaphorically linking co-opetition with music. Then he went
on to explain that a simple, widely understood (among trained
musicians, at least) example of a dominant chord (competitive) resolving to a tonic chord (cooperative),is called the
"perfect authentic cadence." It depicts movement, either from
tension to relaxation or vice versa. It happens when a 5-chord
or dominant chord resolves to a 1-chord, or tonic chord, creating tonality. In other words, perfect dissonance resolves to
perfect consonance.

As composers know, the progressive increases of root to
3rd, root to 5th, and up to root to 11th and root to 13th create more dissonance. Utilizing a chord example of maximum
dissonance, (root to 13th) could become borderline competitionistic—too much competition (chaos) in our equation of
co-opetitive synthesis.

We saw the movie, *Love and Mercy* recently and were reminded of the incredible harmony of maximum dissonance achieved by Brian Wilson of the Beach Boys band of the 1950s, 1960s and beyond. A plethora of other examples of harmonious maximum dissonance abound, such as the works of Stravinsky, Stan Kenton, The Four Freshmen, and many others—all remarkable illustrations of the coopetition always found in music.

We receive pleasure from the harmony of sounds and rhythms. Listening to music triggers in our brains a series of chemical/electrical signals, which in turn stimulates endorphins, adrenaline, depressive or inspiration-producing chemical signals, and a host of other stimuli. In this way, the ordered sounds of music—adapted and modified by man to conform most consistently to the fusion and blending of co-opetitive tones—become like opiates to the brain.

But why does music trigger these stimuli? I postulate that the strike of a pleasing musical chord, or the sounding of exciting rhythms, activates signals in the brain that indicate that life's necessary co-opetitive synthesis has been achieved—or, if there is too much dissonance, that the synthesis is in jeopardy. Well-designed chords and rhythms represent to listening humans a manifestation of the natural synthesis or asymmetric balance of life. We are always intuitively trying to achieve and maintain the best fusion necessary for life. Thus, it is very probable that we invented music in an intuitive attempt to simulate the achievement of co-opetitive synthesis—the feeling of being alive and thriving.

ART AND DESIGN

Music is not the only example of the human expression of the Synthesis: another is visual art in all its manifestations (painting, sculpture, architecture, film, digital, etc.). A design that balances order and chaos is a basic form of art. It is co-opetition, a synthesis of competitive and cooperative forms, designs, colors, and values. Perfect Euclidean forms are generally too orderly and boring to stimulate the eye. They are also a phenomenon not naturally common in our universe, in which circles, squares, and triangles are almost never perfectly shaped.

On the other hand, visual elements that are totally chaotic tend to disturb and can also be either disruptive or unexciting. The synthesis of order and chaos is the foundation of art and design. It is also consistent with an eighteenth-century philosophical definition of beauty, which Scottish moralist and philosopher Frances Hutchinson called "uniformity" (cooperation/order) "in variety" (competition/chaos).

At a prison lecture in *The Tortoise Shell Game*, Anthony Darren, to the delight of the inmates, gets into a debate with Dr. Parsons. The professor and Anthony exchange barbs as they elucidate much of the philosophy discussion in this book. An artist inmate confirms Anthony's theory that much of art is a synthesis of order and chaos. In the year 2000 or so I had the great honor of meeting Dr. Roger Guillemin, winner of the 1977 Nobel Prize and the 1976 Lasker award for discovery of how hormones, including the endorphin, affect brain function. He was the interim President of the Salk Institute. Rather than science, however, he was more interested in talking with me about his computer art. I could see in his amazing artwork the fusion of order and chaos—and we discussed how coopetition synthesis is found in most noteworthy art. I invite your attention to the very cover or dust jacket of this Book. The exploding background of colors and design, not including the outrigger canoe in the foreground, is taken from the digital image, Bestlines, by brilliant artist Ted Packman. It exemplifies a synthesis of order and chaos, both as to the colors and as to design.

Super-imposed in the foreground is the image of the outrigger canoe of the south sea islanders—one of the swiftest boats ever to sail. That canoe is metaphorically very important to this book. Its asymmetric balance symbolizes a smoothly operating capitalist economy. The competition side, consisting of the free-market, liberty, individual rights and a bit of chaos, resides in the main hull. The outrigged pontoon, on the other hand, symbolizes cooperation, i.e. regulation, law and order. The outrigged pontoon is as small and sleek as is necessary to keep the canoe from slowing down, yet large enough so that it serves to prevent the canoe from capsizing in a storm. Thus, co-opetition truly is universal. It is primal; it is ubiquitous.

8

Crime and Freedom

The following discussion is offered as a demonstration of how the theory of co-opetition may be used as a reasoning tool for analyzing any number of diverse issues. The reader is invited to place the tipping point of the synthesis on the sliding scale where he or she thinks it best serves for resolution of the issue. These analyses are meant as examples of the method, not as attempts to prove the relative cogency of a particular argument.

CRIME

Why does the crime rate increase in a society like America has with its relatively high standard of living? We previously discussed how in prehistoric times, human beings developed the ability to survive by being both social and individualistic. Part of being social is to submit or subscribe to leadership and control for the benefit of the group—including oneself. Part of being individualistic is to compete for mates, food, and personal benefits.

Of course, different people have within them different levels of the components of co-opetition. Some individuals lean toward Mother Teresa's side of the scale, others more toward Hitler's. Unfortunately, the intuitive quest for synthesis does not appear to exist at all in some people—the individuals most would call "evil." We will get more into this later, but for now suffice to say that for the sake of pure survival, the human gene pool most likely needs a sprinkling of both the evil and the saintly.

LEADERSHIP

"Leadership" is a co-opetitive word. Leaders are imbued with power (competition) for the benefit (cooperation) of those being led. The benefit would be unity and civility. Therefore, should a vacuum of leadership occur in a complex social setting, a tendency toward social disorder results.

Such disorder can, in turn, lead to an increase in crime. Police states generally offer greater control of crime than do free societies, although at an unacceptable price. On the other hand, in a free society, naïve governmental or family abdication of control, or the break up or dysfunction of the family tend to contribute to increased crime rates.

Relinquishing leadership and worthy role-modeling can lead to the loss of both mutual respect and self-respect, an effect that also contributes to crime. That's why I will often emphasize that although the sort of broad freedom needed to foster truly free competition (individual egoism) is mandatory in a good-working social system, sufficient leadership through laws, family, and culture/tradition/mores is necessary to foster or to enforce cooperation.

Although most people intuitively find the fulcrum point between these desires, others require legal, cultural, moral, and leadership injunctions as a backup to their basic nature. Thus, aside from the always-persistent problem of poverty, we can say that any increase in crime is due partly to the breakdown of culture/ tradition/mores/family. It is also partly due to a misconception by society of what measure of freedom (egoism) should be given to, or taken by, an individual at the expense of the freedoms of others.

In most cultures, it is considered immoral to kill a member of one's own group, but not an enemy. Chronic criminals regard law-abiding members of society as the "enemy." A key to rehabilitating such criminals and to reduce recidivism is to get them to stop regarding the rest of society as the enemy or to somehow get the criminal back on society's team. That said, there will always remain the incorrigible few criminals who are utterly devoid of the basic human qualities suitable for redemption. Such men and women may prove to be pathologically incapable of rehabilitation and releasing them from incarceration may be too dangerous to ever do. Would we turn loose a pack of wild hyenas loose into the streets of society?

On the other hand, after convicted persons pay their debts to society, demonstrate trustworthiness, and prove that their rehabilitation is certain, they must be received back into society and reintegrated onto the human team. For such individuals, the natural urge to cooperate should be tapped and nurtured.

9

Religion and Leadership

RELIGION, PLUS AND MINUS

Pre-Stone Age man had no scientific explanation for why storms blew in, lighting struck, or volcanoes erupted. Man regarded these phenomena as personalities unto themselves. Later, as humans began conquering nature by planting fields and storing grain, they became even more vulnerable to nature's erratic behavior. For newly planted fields, the destructive effects of fire, storms, and pests were much more catastrophic than they were for the wild lands of the nomads.

Having taken steps toward conquering nature, man became less transient and more susceptible to nature's power over his habitat; our ancestors even regarded themselves, at times, as nothing more than prey to nature. This was one reason our ancestors began to pray to nature, to give offerings to her and attempt to cooperate with her.

Religion is a primary example of the cooperative trait. As a result, to this day most of us have faith that some sort of intelligent consciousness started it all—that existence was created with human beings in mind. Without getting into that discussion, the following is intended to be consistent with faith:

Leadership facilitates the coordination of activities within a group. Human beings all have within us, to varying degrees, the urge to subscribe to a teacher, a parent or a leader. To a certain extent everyone feels the urge to be coordinated, protected, and taken care of. Even a highly-placed mortal leader, I believe, has that urge. Thus, the relationship of mortal leaders to spiritual faith is a form of religion—again, an elegant form of cooperation.

In his book *The History of the Decline and Fall of the Roman Empire*, Edward Gibbon argued that Christianity's promise of life after death made the multitudes become non-competitive and useless—or, in my book's interpretation, overly cooperative. Roman citizens lost the fortitude to stave off the invading barbarians, who in contrast took a now-or-never view of life. The Christianized Romans, according to Gibbon, lost interest in the pursuit of both virtue (cooperation) and reward (competition).

A lapse of co-opetition, thus, had much to do with the decline of the Roman Empire. Under the reign of Emperor Trajan in the second century after Christ, Rome reached its zenith of power and dominion. At that time, the empire extended from what is now England through France, Spain, and North Africa into the Middle East, Greece, and the Tigris and Euphrates plains, including the Slavic areas east of the Adriatic Sea, together with a good portion of the Czech, Polish, Germanic, and Teutonic regions.

Next came Emperor Hadrian. Under him, Rome consolidated its territories and did not seek further conquests. Romans enjoyed a one-hundred-year reign of peace. But during this period, they also became increasingly opulent, soft, and corrupt. This was the beginning of the long downward slide. Some few hundred years later, the Empire disintegrated from within and was no longer strong enough to stave off the invading barbarian hordes. Did the Romans forget how to compete, or had the empire become too big to control (because the people were tired of competing), or some of both? There is a strong argument that the Romans became almost entirely dependent on cooperation—i.e. government—and thus co-opetition was lost. I argue that this is one of the reasons Rome eventually failed.

Later, during the so-called Dark Ages, monarchs and feudal lords used religion as a tool for promulgating serfdom. According to this theme, if the serf worked hard and served his feudal master and lord, the serf's goodness, abstinence, and chastity would be rewarded in the afterlife.

In *Darkness and Scattered Light* (1978), William Thompson spoke of a need to "re-mythologize" modern society. Both Thompson's concept of "myth" and Rousseau's concept of nature and "heart" evidence the idea that humankind as a whole has a nature—a soul—which, when allowed to exist free of manmade distortion, has powerfully cooperative characteristics, including faith in God. These characteristics act as governors against the overly-competitive tendencies that are also found in the soul.

Many would argue that even God is co-opetitive. The Bible is full of stories about conflicts between competition and cooperation, and suggestions that the universe and its co-opetitive biophysical properties are themselves the result of God's Invisible Hand.

For example, after Joseph was sold into slavery by his jealous half-brothers, it became known that he had a great powers for interpreting dreams. The king had a dream about seven fat cows followed by seven thin ones, and seven opulent heads of grain followed by seven scorched ones. Joseph predicted seven years of plenty followed by seven years of famine. When he wisely advised the king to store the country's grain during the predicted seven years of plenty, the king made Joseph governor of the entire realm.

Here, government cooperated with the people and protected them from starvation; however, as the king's agent, when the time came Joseph did not just give the grain away. The people who could pay had to buy it. When they ran out of money, they traded their land for the stored food. In other words, they competed. It was a form of co-pay—no utterly free lunch. Famine was avoided. A form of co-opetition prevailed.

10

Happiness and Entertainment

Feeling satisfaction that one has excelled in the art of competing and cooperating for the ultimate synthesis is an intuitive form of happiness. It tells us that our instinctive urge to be productive and to provide for loved ones has been satisfied. This, in turn, means that the urge for reciprocal acknowledgment, respect, love, and appreciation is satisfied. It also means that the feeling of belonging to a group or bonding with others, or of subscription to leadership and team membership, or of experiencing spirituality, is satisfied.

With this in mind, one's happiness should be even greater if this synthesis is attained without one subordinating oneself, but rather, by competing to attain a synthesis for the best possible result for oneself, one's genes, one's group, and their genes. We also expect and hope that the achiever who reaches his goals by playing fairly would be happier than one who achieves similar ends unfairly.

Some happy-seeming reactions to entertainment are in reality nothing but a form of short-lived distraction from the constant quest for synthesis. Attaining co-opetition means more than simply surviving and keeping your head above water. At times entertainment creates an interlude away from stress, but in addition to recharging the body and mind, it may also serve to educate.

In such cases, the experience serves a competitive function by providing concrete rewards. I recently took my grandchildren to see the musical Wicked. My mind was wonderfully primed with the splash of color on stage and the vision of awe on the faces of my grandkids. I slept that night away with the most wondrous of dreams; this gave me respite from the too often sobering realities of life.

This feeling of pleasure, as we now know, results from the release of pleasure-inducing chemicals known as endorphins through the body. This release may be triggered by any number of stimuli, including good feelings that come from giving benefit to others and, conversely, from receiving benefit from others. On a moody day outside on the street, drop some bills into the red kettle as the bells ring, and while you walk away your mind will fill with sunshine.

The act of giving is cooperative, but receiving what is given for oneself or one's group is a form of competition. A synthesis of the two is what creates genuine happiness.

Perhaps the reader can think of other sources of genuine happiness, but I challenge you to find any that do not involve a co-opetitive synthesis.

BULLYING

We've seen the results of unhappiness from verbal bullying: Suicides and nervous breakdowns, among them. Should government get involved with regulating ordinary, non-criminal behavior? Should it police so-called political correctness? No, I don't think so.

But yes, perhaps so in extreme cases, which may be tantamount to common law crimes, mental illness, or the commission of intentional torts or for gross and reckless disregard of potential injury. However, generally, in those incidences we already have in place mechanisms for handling the problem: we have the courts and the law.

Nature has something to do with sibling rivalry, taunting between brothers and sisters, and between teammates. So in general, are kids with brothers and sisters better adjusted than only children? Many passionately argue that a perceived difference is a myth. However, I suspect that the public pressure to achieve zero population growth may color the thinking on this question. Common sense says, everything being equal, there is a difference. Perhaps socialization through peer play could be a compensating factor.

I heard somewhere that if you take a pup away too soon from the litter—from his competing brothers and sisters—it will die. Comedian Don Rickles sometimes assumes the role similar to a bantering sibling; he makes a living putting people down, while getting them to laugh about it.

So, there is a sweet spot between actual bullying and babying that perpetrators should not go beyond, isn't there. In a way, the practice of teasing or kidding may be doing the alleged victim a favor. Being on the receiving end of a certain amount of so-called "bullying" might help him or her mature into a capable adult—

growing from perhaps a proverbial cry-baby into a person more able to cope with life. This has something to do with building character and shaping one into a man or a woman—something the Marine Corps, the military in general, college fraternities, and football teams, among other crucibles, intuitively and quietly all know.

There is good reason for the aphorism "sticks and stones may break my bones, but words can never hurt me." A well-adjusted young person learns spirit, fortitude, perseverance, self-assuredness. So a synthesis between order/cooperation verses chaos/competition must be achieve d. All parties should find the sweet spot for resolving this 'adjustment' issue. Intuitively, won't nature (natural behavior), herself, solve the vast majority of perceived issues?

The incident in November of 2013 involving the Miami Dolphin football team could be a case in point. Controlled aggression on the field is part of the game. Was Mr. Incognito intentionally bullying his teammate, or was he, for the good of the team, intuitively trying to shape his teammate into a more aggressive player? An athlete good enough to play at that level must be very talented athletically, but would he become even better if he played with more aggression? For professional football players, where would you put the synthesis between being too competitive verses being too cooperative?

As we've said, when taunting or character assassination becomes intentionally vicious to the point that harm to the victim is foreseeable or actually occurs, the common law and the courts already have the mechanisms to handle the matter. The government, however, has no business getting more deeply involved with routine behavior control.

I invite you to expand this discussion into the realms of so-called hate speech and political correctness verses freedom of speech and nature's traditional crucibles for shaping character. Keep in mind the idea of allowing nature (auto-functioning co-opetition) to shape and forge a symphonically working society without excessive interference by government.

The TV series "All in the Family" that aired from 1971 through 1979, and a tag-on show picked up through 1983 gave some lessons on the subject. Actor Carroll O'Conner played the role of Archie Bunker, a politically incorrect working family man. We laughed at his bigoted comedy. I feel it took the edges off polarization of the issues of race, ethnicity, religion, gender, and other differences between people. Breaking the tension between polar opposites, as the humor of "All in The Family" did, I believe, led to greater cooperation between disparate groups, and diminished the prejudice and biases between the groups. It did so without government thought police.

Also, it allowed the affected groups to ameliorate by humor the biases between them—to become desensitized. In a way, the show tended to build character and maturity in all parties, including most importantly, that of the audience.

THE WORK ETHIC AND AUTOMATION

The cooperative aspect of group thinking—esprit de corps and mutual assistance, blending with competition between workers—is more likely to promote worker loyalty, and thus good performance to the employer, than would sheer competition between employees. Thus cooperation synthesizes with the competition of individual achievement. Workers striving for higher wages and better working conditions are more likely to achieve a co-opetitive synthesis if they keep in mind their employer's issues and problems as well as their own. The greater the spirit and morale on both sides of the quest for synthesis, the higher the productivity for the company and the greater the increase in standard of living for the worker.

Professor-statistician Dr. W. Edwards Deming, the guru of employee relations in modern manufacturing, shows just how good worker morale can increase quality and a company's productivity and efficiency. In the 1980s, the U.S. lost Dr. Deming for a time to the Japanese. The result was modern Toyota, among others.

If a company becomes extraordinarily successful and registers unusual profits, competition will surely rush in, given no monopoly conditions. On the other hand, when the employee push for ever-growing wages and benefits becomes so great that the employer can no longer compete with other businesses, such is obviously a push too far. The employer might fail and all the employees may lose their jobs. This is why employees are wise to assist, as best they can, their employer in building a thriving business.

Naturally, appreciation and fairness by the boss toward employees fosters good employee morale and is also very important for keeping the business thriving (see *Building the High-Engagement Work Culture: Balancing "Me" with "We,"* David Bowles, PhD, 2011). Dr. Bowles discusses the concept of co-opetition in chapter three of his book, referencing your author's work. One of his favorite examples of co-opetition in nature is that of the elephant seal colonies he came across while traveling in northern California just south of the Big Sur country. The giant male sea mammals would fight among themselves, sometimes to the death, to gain the harem of females. Once the champion bull prevails, though, the others form a protective circle facing outward around the champion and his harem while he mates with each of them.

11

Examples for Potential Application of Co-opetition

The following suggestions do not by any means constitute a comprehensive review of all the available options for each issue discussed. I will show where I believe the sweet spot—the ultimate synthesis point on the scale—should be placed. The reader is encouraged to apply co-opetition to hypothetical scenarios of his or her choosing. Then cross-check your conclusions with people of differing views who have independently applied the theory to the same hypothetical situations. See whether you have drawn closer to one another in understanding and agreement.

"Drawing closer" does not necessarily mean compromise; it means being persuaded by logic to a particular position. In *The Tortoise Shell Game*, Senator Rich Morrison successfully sets up a peace conference when he sends Anthony's book to both U.S.

President Adamson and to communist leader Rodolfo Bramoso; he kept confidential that the other also received a copy.

THE CO-OPETITION CLOCK

Let's illustrate by looking at the face of a clock. That will be our scale. A needle extends upward from the center where the hands are attached. Nine o'clock will represent the far left of the social/political scale, constituting full-on cooperation (voluntary or forced). Conversely, three o'clock will represent the far right of the scale: full-on competition. Noon anchors the center point as the needle arcs over the top of the clock from nine to three o'clock.

IS UTOPIA A GOOD THING?

Saint Thomas More used the word "utopia" in the 1500s, borrowing it from the Greeks. A "utopian" society would be a near-perfect society—no chronic crime, no war, no starvation, no untreated serious mental or physical illness, no poverty, no homelessness, no unhappiness, no suffering—which also means no harm from tsunamis, earthquakes, and volcanoes. It would be a society of full-on cooperation and only the friendliest of competition.

Karl Marx and many others thought they could achieve the utopian ideal here on earth. If that's possible—if we can achieve it—well, why not? What could possibly be wrong with that? Here's a clue. Remember my opening phrase, When earthquakes and volcanoes stop shaking and erupting, life on Earth will quickly end?

Earth's core of molten iron supplies the magma of volcanoes. Upon this core float the continents on their tectonic plates. When the plates grind and bang against each other or split apart, they cause earthquakes and volcanoes—and also build mountains and islands, replenishing the soil that erosion constantly sends to the sea. But most important, the iron core spins, forming a geodynamo that creates a protective magnetic shield over the earth.

This shield, visible in the far north as the aurora borealis, protects life on earth from the deadly solar rays that constantly bombard us. As soon as that iron core cools, it will stop spinning, the aurora will stop her spectacular displays, the magnetic shield will be no more, the atmosphere will boil away due to incoming radiation and life as we know it will end. Earth will become like its dead sister planet, Mars.

With this in mind, do we really want earthquakes, tsunamis and volcanoes to cease their violent behavior? Let's assume for the sake of argument that a utopian society actually came into existence. Would this be a good thing?

As we have learned, to achieve co-opetition in any system or endeavor, elements of competition and cooperation must both be present and unified at the fulcrum of synthesis. Therefore, work and the struggle for survival must be part of the equation. Learning to cope would be a factor. Competing for mates would be a factor. Competing for market share would be a factor. One needs the labor of working up a good sweat, for instance, or exercising one's mental energies, in order to feel good—to feel alive—to feel worthy—to feel accomplished.

Natural selection/competition also comes into play. And we know that it can be unfair and sometimes brutal. But it is there for the survival of the species, isn't it. We know that some diseases filter out genes that would otherwise produce plants and animals incapable of surviving. Further, this type of natural selection could also be a factor contributing to why, every once in a while, a great human genius emerges.

Thus, some strife is a necessary part of life. Some strife is part of the adventure of life. Most humans would define a "reasonable life" as one free of extreme poverty, uncared-for medical needs, crime, and slavery, among others things, but there is an obvious trade-off for making the bubble too secure and too big.

Why not embrace a great part of the challenge? Remember the Hegel quote: "strife is growth." This is one of the reasons for the production of sometimes-exhilarating hormones such as endorphins and adrenaline. It's one of the reasons we are prompted to invent things, to build, to produce art and music, to excel and to perform. It's why a good many people prefer not to vegetate for long periods on the couch watching vacuous television programs.

But as of 2011, American kids were among the most obese children in the world. Some say that's because of too much TV and computer games. Those kids, I fear, have never experienced or were never taught the joy of preparing for the proverbial rainy day. Mother animals start training their young almost from birth. Don't you believe you would feel much better if you knew you were prepared for the storm or the long winter?

If you think about it, do you really want utopia? Certainly you want reasonable fairness of opportunity, but not necessarily fairness of outcome. You want to achieve your own outcome. You want a level playing field, but not a scoreboard rigged in your favor. You want freedom from crime, war, involuntary poverty, and disease. You want to help provide a safety net for those who, due to factors beyond their control, have been brought down to the point where they cannot repair their lives without help.

But you don't want to provide them with a hammock to lounge in. You don't want to give food stamps to someone who will survive by surfing all day—every day—rather than go looking for a job. On national news and TV, we saw the unemployed young adult male surfer in La Jolla, California who'd shamelessly adopted the life-style of living off food stamps and welfare while at the beach every day—all day, happy as a clam. He didn't need to look for a job.

I happened to visit the Braille Institute for the Blind recently and observed young expert, totally sightless teachers training others how to work the various hand-held computer devices, such as I-Phone, Droids, I-pads and similar. I was blown away in amazement. On the wall was the quotation: "You cannot build character and courage by taking away man's initiative and independence. You cannot help men permanently by doing for them what they could do and should do for themselves—Abraham Lincoln."

Too much "utopia" and we become like the wild monkeys at the Costa Rican game preserve. These monkeys were going extinct, the game keepers discovered, because the mothers had forgotten how to teach their young to forage for food. Why? Because the game keepers had been providing food for them. Once that practice ended, nature brought the troop back from the brink of extinction.

The creation of a real utopia would lead mankind out onto a limb that would eventually break off from all the weight—of too many people wishing to be taken care of by their fellow human beings.

At this writing in 2015, fifty percent of the American public pays no income taxes. Of course many such people are in that situation not through their fault , and others have earned their retirement. Still others, however, are gaming the system, voluntarily riding the backs of those who do pay taxes.

Life is not easy, and it is not meant to be easy. Strife is growth. We and our loved ones will inevitably suffer from random events:

fraud, crime, and war; economic recessions, sour business deals, loss of jobs; sickness or injury; divorce, unexpected deaths, accidents; floods, prolonged drought, pestilence, earthquakes, volcanoes, tsunamis, tornados, hurricanes, forest fires, giant solar flares frying the power grid; relatively sudden planet warming or cooling, environmental/biological catastrophe; even asteroid or comet impact, or gamma ray bursts from a supernova created by the death of a giant star.

The earth spins, rotates, and wobbles; it circles the solar system in changing elliptical patterns. Some of those irregularities are responsible for abrupt ice ages and drastic climate changes, including abrupt desertification and drought. Remember: sixty-five million years ago, a giant meteor struck the earth in the vicinity of the Yucatan peninsula, Mexico, ending the age of the dinosaur and launching the reign of the mammals.

If the human species hopes to prevail on earth for much longer, it must be in constant training for such changes. We must keep or regain our edge, both mentally and physically. It is not necessary to train the way the Navy SEALs train, but more like the result of participation in high-school sports, youth camps, adult conditioning—even walking and brain-expanding hobbies.

Parents should teach their young that life is a constant effort to keep one's head above water. It is an effort to keep the heads of your family members above water. It helps if you prepare yourself to better handle it. It helps if you can build a raft to float on, especially for old age. But even then, you would need some protection from too many others climbing aboard and sinking your family or your senior raft—as by redistributing your assets and resources. If everyone to the best of his abilities, however, builds his own raft, such would be best for all.

I will later show how nature can help us do this. I will show how building more and bigger rafts will raise all ships, and contribute to building even more rafts for those with nothing on which to float.

What's more, humans must constantly push the envelope of education and knowledge. And yes, a social safety-net is essential—but surely not the hammock. Too much cooperation— forced or otherwise—and not enough competition, and the human species will quickly perish from this earth. It will become a tiny flash in the archeological pan. The bubble of dependence built by good-hearted but naïve achievers will burst, leaving the human race vulnerable to extinction. In this way, utopia would insidiously lead to stagnation and death.

Instead, the human being should become expert at the art of living; this includes harmonizing cooperation and competition into the ultimate synthesis of co-opetition. In the 2011 Woody Allen–directed film *Midnight in Paris,* the character Mary laments the loss of the glories of the previous age, to which Gil responds that each age is a little "unsatisfying, because life is a little unsatisfying." But that is what keeps us striving and living, isn't it? Dissatisfaction. No strife, no edge.

But of course, too much strife does not result in a good life either. So where is the tipping point, the sweet spot? I place the achievement of utopia at an undesirable 10:30 on the co-opetition scale. On the other hand, to achieve a good, low-crime, free-market democratic society, one that enjoys a status of liberty for all, the synthesis point would be placed somewhere between 1:00 and 1:15. Again, recall that co-opetition is not a pure balance; it is a chord whose harmony requires some dissonance. The balance is, therefore, asymmetric. Within reason, humankind should adapt (cooperate) and cope (compete) with adversity—including earthquakes, tsunamis, and volcanoes.

THE NANNY STATE

How many times have we heard something we already know from our innate primal wisdom: that God (and Nature) helps those who help themselves? But our primal wisdom also tells us that those who, through no fault of their own, are incapable of surviving and helping themselves, or who are retired and have already done their share, should be protected by some form of social safety net. However, when regarding the lazy, the scammers, and those who live by leeching off others, our primal wisdom says we should help them with only bare essentials and basic healthcare.

Don't wheel the aid to their front door. Require them to go get it, and perhaps look for a job along the way. Primal wisdom does not urge us to give them a hammock, car or TV, or supply them with booze or casino gambling money. Does your wisdom require such uber-cooperation?

Survival is the basic demand of nature, and survival requires some competition—some effort—effort from all living things. If you are capable of pulling your weight but put forth no effort, you become a drag on everyone else, and the economy sinks. Not only does that suppress general happiness, but it could lead eventually to the premature extinction of humankind.

Many argue that an alarming trend persists in the states of New York and California, to name only two. Call it becoming hooked on dependency. Are politicians lately more brazen about handing out benefits and other subsidies to voters, seemingly to make their lives easier, but in reality to "buy" votes? Perhaps the press will see the danger of this trend and illuminate it. As we know, one of the bastions of freedom and democracy is an objective, unbiased media.

Merging order with chaos, and finding the proper point of synthesis between them, will enable the natural synergism of the forces within the economy to work. Such will offer the best chance to naturally open the floodgates and fill the lake of prosperity. Then, as all ships rise, the 47 percent of non-taxpayers will exponentially shrink. Hopefully, the shrinkage will reach as low as 25 percent? A side-effect should be a concomitant rise in happiness and knowledge.

RE-CULTURALIZATION AND RE-MYTHOLOGIZING

Traditionally, the egoistic, competitive traits of individuals in society are tempered by moralities and conventions that support both group and personal benefit. But these old systems, whether religious/spiritual or nonreligious, often lag behind the ever faster lifestyle changes of the modern world.

Along with good old rationality, I propose that a form of cultural "retooling"—re-adopting time-tested mythologies and spiritualism, religions, culture, and ethics into modern life—could and should be encouraged. Such encouragement should not be a governmental function—horrors—but rather be drawn primarily from family traditions and, in particular, from the efforts of the thinkers, writers, professors, teachers, clergy, philosophers, pundits, screenwriters, playwrights, artists, critics, television and film producers and directors, composers, lyricists, musicians, toy and game producers, advertisers, cartoonists, journalists, talk-show hosts, a discerning public, perceptive parents—and perhaps most of all, a persistent, diligent, objective, ethical press and media.

What's more, there is something universally appropriate and natural about promulgating the virtues of family, love, honor, respect, honesty, charity, credibility, reliability, manners, ethics, self-reliance, industriousness, leadership, and accomplishment. Bring back the strength of the family as a primary factor in all of that; again, trust Mother Nature to work her magic. The family status, for those who have the desire for it, is the more natural state.

Karl Marx believed the family was becoming obsolete. My impression was that he implied "good riddance." I believe that the disintegration of the family is leading to the disintegration of society as a whole, to the severe detriment of the human species. At this point in history in the U.S., I judge our fulcrum on the synthesis scale for these virtues should be placed at around noon. Unfortunately in many respects, the needle is pushed too far to the left into the government-dependence extreme—to, say, 10:30. Or else it is pushed too far to the right into the egoism extreme—to about 2:30.

What do I mean by that? I refer to kids being abandoned, parents not being honored, unnecessary abortions stemming from pure selfishness. I'm by no means talking about all abortions of course. Revitalizing the culture of family would, by itself, recapture much lost ground. With the breakdown of the family, has come much of the ills of modern society: astronomically high out-of-wedlock births, increasing poverty, increasing crime, abandonment of old folks—including elderly former wives and mothers.

The black family is especially jeopardized; far fewer fathers now feel the family is their responsibly than did in the past. The loss of such traditions increases the necessity for government welfare and elderly entitlements—if not for entitlements for all. This in turn leads to unintended consequences: the creation of a dependent society.

The road to hell is paved with good intensions. Without curtailing a women's right to be a/the breadwinner, bring back the old traditions of stay-at-home moms and discourage husbands and fathers from abandoning the marriage. I strongly suggest favoring tax laws that bring families together to counter government policies that drive them apart; favor policies that reward and encourage adult children to take care of grandpa and grandma and other family dependents so they'd be less dependent on social security. Eliminate or discourage or rewrite all tax regulations or welfare programs that work against the promulgation of the family and marriage.

We knew all this when Bill Clinton, at the insistence of his Republican Congress, and to his credit, signed the Welfare Reform Act of 1996 (known as the Personal Responsibility and Work Opportunities Act). Dramatic improvements happened almost overnight. Bill Clinton's welfare reform act was designed to reduce dependency on welfare. One way to accomplish that was to adopt policies that strengthened the family and promoted responsibility of parents, especially the father.

According to the House Ways and Means Committee, "The major goal of Public Law 104–193 is to reduce the length of welfare spells by attacking dependency while simultaneously preserving the function of welfare as a safety net for families experiencing temporary financial problems." The bill's primary requirements and effects included aiming to encourage two-parent families and discourage out-of-wedlock births.

The act emphasized a shift towards work, with names such as "Workfare" and "Work First." Between 1997 and 2000, enormous numbers of the poor left or were terminated from the program, with a national drop of 53 percent in total recipients. The improving trend continued as of 2006. See "Welfare Reform Turns Ten: Evidence Shows Reduced Dependence, Poverty." By Christine Kim and Robert Rector.

This improving trend lasted until the present democrat administration began in January 2009. This administration has by edict recently placed loopholes into the 1996 reform act. More states can now choose not to require "workfare" under certain conditions. Coincidentally, the poverty rate has skyrocketed.

Did the loopholes come because of changing poverty rate, or did the increasing poverty rate cause the loopholes? Was this because of the administration's policies, was it the result of the 2009 Great Recession, was it attributable to the handling or lack of handling of the economy since then, was it a cultural sea change, or was it a combination of all the above?

As of 2013, the country is worse off than it has ever been. The proportion of people on food stamps has increased exponentially. Even more disconcerting, however, are recent trends in the poverty rate. Poverty has now increased for four successive years, resulting in the addition of approximately 10 million people to the U.S. poverty population since 2006.

More than 46 million people were officially "poor" in 2010, which is the highest total since the Census Bureau started measuring poverty in 1959. More people have become poor since 2009 than during any other presidential term for which there is data.

How does this relate to the family unit? "The Black Family Is Worse off Today Than in the 1960s," headlines Your Black World Coalition, according to a report released by the Urban Institute (March 2013).

Among many other things, it shows that 71 percent of black births are out of wedlock. It is very high for whites too. In part the report states: ". . . The government took away the black man's power by taking away his responsibility to his family . . . made to uplift themselves the American power structure went out of its way to destroy it." This obviously is about welfare's disincentives for family, and about government policies that foster dependency.

The increasing trend of single or divorced women in later years having no security is a factor that may cause them to want to metaphorically "marry" the federal government. In this way they gain a "breadwinner" that will provide entitlements. To discourage that tendency, encourage the voluntary spread of much of the responsibility of taking care of dependents and the elderly to where it traditionally belonged—to the family. After all, Honor Thy Mother and Father is the Fifth Commandment—from many thousands of years of tradition.

In *The Tortoise Shell Game*, Anthony strives throughout the saga to put his family together. Does he succeed?

STABILITY OF GOOD GOVERNMENT

Good operating governance is preferred and should be set at 12:55 on the scale. Unstable local governments are prone to develop into unstable countries, They, in turn, may become subject to revolution, become aggressive to neighbors, start stampedes of refugees, or become disruptive to world peace and a well-functioning world economy.

However, I emphasize the term good government when I say this. Should a government operate so far out of balance that synthesis is irretrievable, perhaps little good comes from attempting to prop it up. Let it fall of its own weight—but only if the subsequent government would be better than the failed one.

Examples of going from the preverbal frying pan into the fire abound: the Muslim Brotherhood gaining power in Egypt through democratic means, then within a few months effectively outlawing democracy and adopting a theocracy; the demise of Saddam Hussein and Omar Kaddafi and winding up with ISIS, (although in the Iraq case a two–year period of control prevailed, but security troops were prematurely withdrawn.); in the early 1900s, the Red

Army commandeering the Russian Revolution from the White Russians; Castro commandeering the Cuban revolution from his co-revolutionaries; Hugo Chavez commandeering change in Venezuela and essentially ending the free press; socialist-fascist-Hitler commandeering German unrest; Mao taking over Tibet; the Ayatollah Khomeini taking over Iran; and many others.

In Cuba's case, at the time of the revolution, I was a first-year law student in Los Angeles, having just majored in political science and economics in college. Castro was on his victory march across Cuba on the way to Havana. In the beginning there was great empathy all over the world for his cause. Fulgencio Batista was, to say the least, a hated man. But as Castro progressed along his victory march he stopped at every town and village and, with no trial or hearing, lined up and executed multitudes of people.

That behavior was inconceivable to me as a young student of the law. By the time Fidel arrived in Havana, people's minds had completely changed about him. Despite his initial denials, he proved to be a Communist, where the motto is: The ends justify the means.

The shocking realization of his despotic conduct eventually shook even Hollywood, which had looked the other way when his supporters began hijacking airliners and flying them to Cuba. It became bloodily obvious that the Castro collectivists had no regard for individualism. For Cuba, the synthesis scale fell all the way to 9:00. Today it is probably at about 10:00, but it needs to be at 1:00 or higher before Cuba can rise to a state worthy of her beauty, people, culture, music, and ambience.

In *The Tortoise Shell Game*, the rebels—headed by General El Gato Pascalle—were fighting a revolution against communist dictator Rudy Bramoso, and the issue was whether they could reach a synthesis, a cease fire. The white swirls of the marble conference table between them illustrated the synthesis. The merger of the individual, competitive, chaotic eddies within the orderly and cooperative black background of the table-top provided a beautiful image of co-opetition. The white eddies depicted individual rights, civil rights, but the black background symbolized societal and collective interests.

A free market system with a democratic constitutional republic-type government is the preferred vehicle for synthesizing the opposites; that stability depends upon maintaining the synthesis—knowledge Castro could have benefited from. Of cardinal importance is a constitution or charter that protects the civil rights of all, including the minority (rich or poor, white or black), a constitution that protects the minority from tyranny of the majority.

On the one hand, those governments that are controlled by collectivists and/or theocracies to the complete disregard of individualism and civil rights, including free speech and freedom of religion must be regarded as out of synthesis.

On the other hand, individualism that abuses the rights of other members of society, as I said, whether they are the minorities, the poor, the rich, the workers, the women, or any other, also creates imbalance. These are the reasons for constitutional rules against unequal protection of the law, against lack of due process, against discrimination. Evidence of these abuses is proof that synthesis has not been reached.

Stability can be provided by finding the point of synthesis between the power of the masses and that of an influential elite of society. Finding and maintaining that point cannot be achieved without putting into operation a well thought-out constitution or government charter. I believe that attempting to reach a tipping point at somewhere between 12:45 and 1:30 on the scale is a good start for maintaining the synthesis of a stable government.

Further, a proper charter is crucial to an emerging government; it must provide for the human rights of the individual, the dissenter, and the egoist. The U.S. Bill Of Rights is the prime example. Then to synthesize those rights with the needs and demands of the group, the General Welfare Clause of the Constitution is an example. (That clause states that Congress can tax and spend to benefit the general welfare of the nation. This concept will be further illustrated in the later sections on political systems.) That formula should include free opportunity (not guaranty) for individuals to work and earn their way up the economic ladder.

However, once again I feel obliged to underscore the important caveat that emphasis must be placed on synthesis rather than mere balance. Synthesis most often is an asymmetric balance. Balancing the opposites without synthesis will not accomplish coopetition. To achieve synthesis is to exercise reason and not submit to mere compromise. Use reason to achieve a meaningful compromise without giving up good faith rational principles.

Without synthesis, special interests at each extreme can crowd out the interests of the less vocal but hardworking people in the middle. The special interests seeking unrestrained egoism on one side or government-protected advantage on the other do not properly synthesize the rights and needs of the people in the middle. Who speaks for them? Who lobbies for them?

Examples of opposite extremes would include, on the one hand, subsidies of undeserved corporate welfare, and on the other hand, government handouts that reward those who game the system and take from it more than their share. It includes inefficient, unnecessary bureaucracies that maintain themselves in power and compensation. The public of any emerging country should be wary that those on each extreme may/will/do scratch one another's backs, using the legislature to take from the middle class and give to the extremes.

ROOM FOR IMPROVING U.S. LAWS AND PROTECTIONS

We've heard the lament: "Too big to fail?" If so, such is strong evidence that the entity in question is ipso facto already a monopoly. Antitrust regulators should investigate, and if violations are provable, prosecute and break up the company. Instead, we have to live with government-protected monopolies. Worse, you can bet that government-cronyism had a part in them becoming too big to fail in the first place.

The inane excuse given by the big national company is that foreign companies are even bigger, so to compete, the big national company has to grow even bigger than that. They may also argue that foreign companies are unfairly subsidized by their countries. There are ways of addressing and solving those issues that are too numerous to detail at this point; suffice to say that claims before the World Trade Organization or threats of tariffs are a start.

On that "too big to fail" issue, the synthesis scale is currently at 2:00 and should be moved back to 12:30.

Any number of other distortions of the cooperative impulse exemplify this "too big to fail" inequity: The bailout of Wall Street and the big banks after the financial crises of 2009; most big farm subsidies; the bailout of General Motors, which benefitted mostly its unions so they could preserve their member's bloated pensions—pensions that were largely responsible for bringing that giant to its knees in the first place.

The road to hell is paved with good intentions. Instead of receiving a bailout, the first route taken should have been Chapter 11 bankruptcy protection. But instead of allowing the courts to properly honor the traditional priority rights of bond-holder creditors over union pensions and employee benefits, the U.S. government engineered the reverse result—against the principles of common law priorities and the laws of bankruptcy.

As of 2013, the extent of the GM bondholder losses is still uncertain. They were relegated to lowly shareholder status in the reorganized company—their shares, therefore, worth probably 30 cents on the dollar as of 2013. No wonder potential investors, in general, are leery and the economy as of 2015 remains weak. Only Wall Street seems to flourish while floating on the lowest interest rates in history. The latter was due in large part to the Fed's—Federal Reserve Banks—artificial "quantitative easing"—another term for "printing more money"; it also created another giant economic bubble that's waiting to burst.

If the GM bond holders had been paid in accordance with traditional priorities of law, they would have more likely become candidates for legitimate reinvestment into other parts of the economy—such as in residential mortgages. Instead, for whatever reason, the unions who've contributed hundreds of millions into selected campaigns received priority protection or payment of their pensions, senior to the bondholders.

The national economic recovery as of 2015 still suffers, and according to AOL Jobs as of April 2013, the real unemployment rate is an unwieldy 11.7 percent. AOL Jobs includes those on disability who want jobs, and those whose unemployment checks ran out who also want jobs. ("The Real Unemployment Rate Is Worse Than You Think." Claire Gordon, posted Apr 5th 2013). In April 2013, unemployment in California was at 9.8 percent, the nation's highest of the fifty states. It is the highest rate since California became a state in 1850. If the figures included the disabled who want to work, those who've given up looking, and those now relegated to part-time jobs, the unemployment rate in California would be up around 14 percent.

In Detroit, Michigan, a city people have been leaving in droves, unemployment in 2013 was 21 percent according to the U.S Bureau of Labor Statistics; the real rate would be much higher. Detroit filed for municipal bankruptcy in 2013. What does all the above mean? It means that those who've become dependent on the protection of a bubble—the union wage-protection/benefits-bubble, the bailout bubble, the government hand-out bubble, and the forced-cooperation bubble—can't handle adversity when it arrives and the bubble actually bursts.

Interestingly, Ford Motor Company didn't take all the bailouts that GM gobbled up, yet Ford is doing comparatively better. It obviously did a better job competing in the marketplace rather than relying so much on the cooperation of government assistance.

These are cases of unintended consequences resulting from government interference, in this case from bailouts and labor protection. In my view, such interference under the federal administration in 2015 ranks at 10:30 on the synthesis scale, while the synthesis should be placed at about 1:00.

Between these opposite extremes lie those individuals and businesses who keep their heads down, don't ask for special advantages, and don't have the time for activism, but just continue to work and produce and synergistically keep the economy going—and pay almost all the taxes. Those are the persons most needed for achieving co-opetition. Perhaps that vast middle majority of producers is the most underrepresented of any constituency in the industrial economies, yet it is no doubt the most valuable resource any country could enjoy.

FIRE ON THE FLOOR

For more than thirty-five years, the virtual police state of Egypt's Hosni Mubarak provided a painful illustration of the effects of involuntary cooperation. The regime tolerated very little dissent or freedom. The seemingly spontaneous eruption of the February 2011 revolution came in good part from competition by individuals seeking basic human rights and freedoms. So, on the one hand, we see involuntary cooperation forced by the state. On the other hand, we see the competition by individuals for freedom and liberty. Unfortunately, wild and chaotic expressions of freedom can inadvertently put fire on the floor. Expressions of freedom based on reason and wisdom place fire in the hearth. Fire in the hearth is co-opetition. Fire on the floor leads to burning down the house.

The hearth is a metaphor for a great constitution. In 2011 I wrote: "Let us hope that the transition of the Egyptian fire of revolution to fire in a well-designed hearth will be attained. Such a fireplace is one that will allow freedom to reign without too much danger of its being extinguished by factions bent on commandeering the government for their own ends. The hearth should be built so that the fire-hose of tyranny can never reach the flames within it."

Now in 2015, we see that the fire escaped the hearth in Egypt and landed on the floor. As alluded to earlier, the first thing Morsi and the Muslim Brotherhood did when they gained leadership and supposedly re-installed democracy and freedom was to change the nation's constitution to effectively eliminate those very things. They essentially instituted a theocracy! Many of us had believed that theocracies went out with the end of the dark ages.

Look what happened to Italian philosopher-Dominican friar-mathematician Giordano Bruno in 1600. He'd proclaimed that earth revolved around the sun, that the stars and the sun were one and the same genus, and that a universe existed out there. The inquisitionists burned him at the stake. Look what happened to Galileo and his telescope. He was thrown in irons by the Inquisition for most of the rest of his life.

Thus, Egypt slid from the proverbial frying pan into the fire. The trump card for democracy in that country, however, was the military, which soon jailed the new leadership for violation of the freedoms of the people.

The U.S.'s analogy to that was the American Revolution in 1776, where the Founders symbolically jailed the King of England and fought to gain democracy. If some of our revolutionaries had afterward attempted to commandeer the newly gained democracy and turn it into a theocracy, I am sure they would have been hanged at dawn, or George Washington would have climbed back on his horse. In a way, this leads us to the next subject, gun control. I will show the connection.

GUN CONTROL

The right to protect our children from people wielding guns. The right to protect our church parishioners from a lunatic gun-wielding hate monger.

None of us want our children exposed to the danger of another Newtown, Connecticut—another Sandy Hook Elementary, or another South Carolina black church massacre. It is our right and duty to make sure that our children, churches, and our schools are absolutely safe—in fact that we are all safe. We must protect ourselves from potential mass murderers. The tragedy of losing a child or a loved one at the hands of a gun wielding perpetrator is beyond comprehension. The mentally ill, the violent criminal, the terrorist, the negligent, and the child too young to understand the danger, do not have the right to bear arms, whether under the 2d Amendment of the U.S. Constitution, or not.

The right to bear arms. On the other hand, the right to bear arms under the 2nd Amendment of the U.S. Constitution is not merely for hunting deer; it is to allow citizens to protect themselves, and to protect the U.S. Constitution—by force if necessary. The right to bear arms came as a natural right to our shores from antiquity. The right was confirmed from time to time, culminating in an old concession forced upon the King of England in the 1600s. There are sobering things to consider before we go down the path of disarming the people. The people have always been suspicious of a standing army under the total control of a king, ruler, or powerful leader.

Reconciling these two rights. How can finding the correct synthesis of co-opetition help us resolve this issue?

The Constitution is the supreme law of the land, and in that regard is sacred. We are not generally aware, however, that the 2nd Amendment right—and all constitutional rights to a greater or lesser extent—could be lost, and perhaps very quickly. Those rights are vulnerable. For instance, it could happen if a catastrophic terrorist attack hits our shores again sometime in the future—no matter who is President at the time.

I'll tell you why. As Commander-in-Chief, the President, presumably with the consent of Congress, has the power to invoke martial law. What does that mean? It means that under extreme circumstances, a form of military rule may be legally declared by the President. At that moment, a military dictatorship substitutes in place of democracy. Something akin to that is what just happened in Egypt by the military unseating the Muslim Brotherhood. This could happen here overnight.

It could happen under the authority of Article 1, Section 9, and Clause 2 of the Constitution. That clause allows Congress to suspend the writ of habeas corpus. That writ generally provides that no one can be arrested and held more than a few days without a court order showing there is reasonable cause to hold the person. The authorities must show that it is probable that the person committed a crime or is otherwise subject to the court's control.

A suspension of that writ of habeas corpus means that the President—the executive branch of the government—temporarily becomes a military dictator, supposedly for the good of the country. In that way, the President imposes military rule over civil rule. President Lincoln did it with the authority of Congress for five years during the Civil War in the 1860s.

However, in the case of Milligan v U.S., Lincoln's usurpation of power eventually—meaning for five years—was declared unconstitutional by the Supreme Court. The court said that: "Martial law . . . destroys every guarantee of the Constitution." The Court reminded us that such actions—suspension of rights and of habeas corpus—were taken by the King of Great Britain, which in part, led to the American Revolution.

"Civil liberty and this kind of martial law cannot endure together; the antagonism is irreconcilable; and, in the conflict, one or the other must perish," the court said. The court ruled further that martial rule can never exist where the courts are open, and in the proper and unobstructed exercise of their jurisdiction. Moreover, the court confined any martial takeover to the locality of an actual war. But our leaders did not always follow those restrictions on martial law.

During the Second World War, American-born and naturalized citizens of Japanese descent on the west coast of the U.S.—over 100,000 people—were interned under a form of declaration of martial law—.i.e., the suspension of habeas corpus. Many years later, the U.S. Congress apologized and paid reparations of over 1.2 billion dollars.

Nevertheless, the people of other countries are not always as careful and protective of their freedoms as are many Americans. There have been well-known disastrous consequences. In the 1930s, after years of being deprived of economic security by depression and inflation, the people of Germany became demoralized.

The Nazi Party secretly took advantage by burning the Parliament building in Berlin. The Nazi-dominated coalition government blamed the fire on Communists, propagandizing it as Communist Party terrorism, giving the Nazis a pretext for their next step, their declaration of martial law. They suspended all civil liberties, including, specifically, habeas corpus. A few weeks later, the Nazis persuaded Parliament to surrender its power through the infamous Enabling Act, under which the Parliament allowed the Chancellor to rule by decree. The Chancellor did so for 12 more years. The world then had to rid itself of Chancellor Adolf Hitler.

But ask yourself what would happen in the U.S. under the following scenario: a horrendous terrorist act causes martial law to be declared—that is, the President, whoever he or she is at the time, suspends the writ of habeas corpus. Let's say he/she later abuses his takeover and never ends martial law. It might take months or even years for a case to be heard before the U.S. Supreme Court (as in Lincoln's case). What would happen if that hypothetical power-grab is not rescinded after a reasonable period? You remember the phrase "absolute power corrupts absolutely?" Perhaps that syndrome causes the delay.

The people of the U.S. would have the right to object to the abuse of martial law—like what happened in Iran in 2009 when the young people revolted. But the protesting Iranians had no guns, and the protest was brutally suppressed. People were killed. People disappeared. However, in the U.S., citizens have a last bulwark, a last chance to exercise their protests and defend themselves against false arrest...they have the right to bear arms. They have assault weapons locked in their closets and basements.

An interesting and very controversial American case in point is The People v Sagon Penn. Thirty years or so ago in San Diego, one police officer was killed and a few others, including a female ride-along, wounded in the line of duty. The officers were trying to arrest Sagon Penn, an African-American black belt martial artist. It turned out later that they had the wrong guy.

Mr. Penn disarmed one officer and used the gun to kill and wound the others. Attorney Milton Silverman successfully defended Penn, primarily on the grounds of self-defense. The police had unknowingly tried to arrest the wrong man—a man they did not have probable cause to arrest. Penn was acquitted of murder at his first trial, but the jury deadlocked on manslaughter charges. A second jury acquitted him of attempted murder and manslaughter charges, but deadlocked on lesser charges. He was not tried again. The police were not happy about that. Many years later in 2002, Penn died where he lived with his mother, allegedly from suicide.

But here's the point of the case: presumably, citizens have the right to resist false arrests. Do citizens have the right to resist arrests resulting from a persistent illegal state of martial law, from an illegal suspension of the writ of habeas corpus, from a totalitarian takeover that has turned bad and become an illegal power-grab? Under those circumstances, isn't it consistent with logic that the people should also have the right to bear arms in order to protect themselves from illegal arrest and suspension of habeas corpus? Until there is a more definitive ruling on this hypothetical issue, it would seem that citizens could at least fire their weapons in provable, legal, self-defense.

But there is no way to tell in advance whether any hypothetical suspension of habeas corpus has festered to the point of becoming illegal. It could be argued that it is not illegal until a court of law rules it as such. This is the archetypal Catch 22. Which comes first, the illegality, or a court order ruling a particular act illegal?

Here is the important point: the prospect of citizens using firearms in self-defense would make a potential abuser of the power of martial law think twice before truly abusing that power. If the Ayatollah of Iran had a country full of citizens with guns in their closets to think about, perhaps his repression of democratic protests would have had a different result.

The 2014, riots and protests in Kiev, Ukraine also exemplify Government-guns against citizen's-rocks. The government would think twice before abusing its power if guns were to be potentially answerable with guns in self-defense rather than answered with rocks.

On the other hand, when Russian tanks later invaded the Ukrainian Crimean peninsula, domestic armed citizen protests would not seem to offer any match at all against that overwhelming power. If the citizens had guns locked in their closets, however, such may have caused the Russians to think twice before invading.

Perhaps that potential is the very reason countries like Switzerland require males between the ages of 20 and 34 to keep automatic weapons and ammunition locked in their homes. Military service and reserves are mandatory in Switzerland. And we note that the rate of accidental shootings, gun crime and homicide is very low there as compared with the U.S.

Don't misunderstand the premise here. I would fully and legally resist anyone from attempting to violently overthrow the government of the United States—a gross violation of law. Someday, though, the courts will have to decide whether citizens have the right of self-defense in circumstances where the government illegally abuses its power and unlawfully shuts down freedom.

Does the right of self-defense remain in situations where illegal government abuse forces the citizens to defend themselves? Thus, many would argue that the 2d amendment right should be amended; that the citizens should blindly trust the government to not abuse its power. Others argue that they keep their guns locked in their closets because the constitution philosophically trusts they will not irrationally use them and abuse their right to bear arms, or it trusts that they will use them only in self-defense or to protect the constitution. The question remains: may they bear their guns in self-defense, perhaps even from illegal government abuse?

In the 2008 case of District of Columbia v Heller, the court struck down a gun control law as unconstitutional. The court said, in part, that the 2nd Amendment to the Bill of Rights was originally enacted largely because the Antifederalists feared that the Federal Government would disarm the people in order to disable the citizens' militia. The court said the Founders were fearful that this would empower a politicized standing army or select militia to rule. Their response to the federalists was to deny Congress the power to abridge the ancient right of individuals to keep and bear arms; in this way, the ideal of a citizens' militia would be preserved.

A reasonable inference to draw from that court ruling is that if martial law ever is imposed and abused—for example, never rescinded—the people's militias could conceivably pit themselves against the federal army to help protect the rights guaranteed under the U.S. Constitution. This could plausibly occur, for example, if a tyrant suspended habeas corpus and declared himself a dictator.

It happened in Germany. It happened in Iran. It happened in North Korea. It happened in Libya. It happened in other parts of Africa. It happened in Cuba and several more times in Latin America. It happened for a few months in Egypt. It happens just about everywhere a dictator commandeers control of a democracy.

And it conceivably could happen some day in the U.S. In the Heller case, the court further ruled that the term "well-regulated militia" meant no more than that the gun owner should be trained to handle firearms, and the court had precedent to back up that ruling. For example, in *The Tortoise Shell Game*: The dictator Rodolfo Bramoso refused to negotiate with the rebels until they laid down their arms. El Gato, the rebel general, knew he would lose his leverage if he acceded to that demand. You will see how that plays out under the concept of the synthesis.

As a side note, other countries and entities exist that are capable of smuggling arms to protestors in, say, Iran, Libya, Syria, or Egypt. It is assumed that the CIA has at times served in that role. But if the citizens of the entire world, including those of the U.S., are ever disarmed, there would be no source to supply weapons for a meaningful protest through self-defense.

For argument, let's say that American citizens are disarmed and the rest of the world is also disarmed. Now assume that martial law for some reason is imposed here and never rescinded—in that case, what country or source would be capable of coming to the aid of the protesting citizens of the U.S.? What group would supply arms? Only if weapons are already in the hands of the people would the rulers fear or think twice about abusing a state of martial law.

At the United Nations, there is talk about disarming all the peoples of the world—except for standing armies. This might be fine if the United Nations could insure that no despot or dictator would ever again usurp the right of the people to self-govern. Many at the U.N. think they can accomplish that under a World Government. Surely they are kidding themselves. World government means no individual nations, no competition in the co-opetition equation.

It is illuminating to note who in history was pro-gun, and who disarmed the people. All the dictators and collectivists of the past disarmed their people—Hitler, Stalin, Mao, Castro, Hugo Chavez, Pol Pot, and Mussolini, to name the most infamous. All the advocates of freedom were pro-gun—including, you might be surprised to learn, the Dalai Lama, Indira Gandhi, and George Orwell.

On the other hand, it is hard to argue against the apparent success of the Australian model: generally, Aussies ban weapons in the hands of private citizens. However, although reports are mixed, gun crime seems not to have gone down. Suicides, yes—but not murders.

The evidence is mixed when we compare the U.S. to the U.K. Although murders with guns are much higher in the U.S., violent crime, assaults and home invasions in the U. K. are reported to be much higher, per capita, than in the U.S. Could it be that in the U.S., perpetrators of that sort of crime are dissuaded by the probability that a prospective victim might have a weapon in his house?

Let's talk about another interesting phenomenon: Why is it that massacres from non-military perpetrators occur even in gun-free countries or gun-free zones? Could it be because when no guns are around from which to shoot back, the situation becomes more attractive to lunatics and terrorists? In 1996 in Britain, 16 children and one adult were slaughtered. In Germany in 2009, 16 students were killed in a single incident. Recently, the worst shooting massacre of young people in history—69 lives gone, 110 wounded—occurred in Norway. These countries are all gun-free zones. Interestingly, the Aurora, Colorado shooter—the nut who thought he was the Joker of Batman lore—chose to attack the only theatre in the area that posted a "gun-free" sign.

Why is it that the children of privileged Washington journalists and politicians, for the most part, go to private schools defended by armed guards? Yet they want the rest of us to trust a gun-free zone, or a gun-free city, a gun-free state . . . or even a gun-free nation.

We should also not forget that in times of public crises, such as sometimes arise during storms, riots, wars or other calamities, individuals often truly need guns to protect their families. In the scenario of a natural disaster—or any disaster—we might need protection from marauders seeking to take more than an offered, charitable share of our food, our generators, our water, medical supplies, or shelter. In the spirit of full disclosure, presently I don't personally own a gun, but I appreciate that a neighbor or two of mine might own one.

Regardless of the Australian model, spoken of above, the U.S is unique. In this country, there appears to be good reason to synthesize the demands of the individual for preservation of freedom with a need for ultimate protection from negligence, nuts, criminals, terrorists, and despots.

So how do we reconcile the right to protect our children with the right to bear arms? Both rights are equally important. We are intelligent beings. We should be capable of figuring this out. Let's apply the theory of co-opetition to the problem. The act of disarming the public is, in substance, one of government forcing cooperation upon the people. On the other hand, to continue living with all sorts of guns and no safeguards is to allow individual competition to reign beyond reason. A synthesis of these two behavioral forces must be found. Some thoughts:

It's not practical to disarm all people in the U.S. In the first place, there are some 200 million guns in the hands of the U.S. public. Counting law enforcement weapons, about 300 million guns exist for 315 million people. From a pragmatic standpoint, how could you disarm all those people, even if you wanted to? Embarking on such a course could very possibly breed a police state. Some citizens would readily give up their freedom and liberty to such a state, believing the government would offer the best protection for them. By analogy—"better red than dead" was the mantra of such people during the Cuban missile crisis. But most people would never willingly give up their liberty and freedom. Would you?

For immigrants or those not familiar with our culture in the U.S., the thirst of Americans for freedom would be difficult to fathom. I don't know whether a hunger for freedom can be taught. I suspect it must be lived to be fully appreciated and cherished. The normal state of relative freedom verses restriction of liberty for most other people of the earth has been historically that of overwhelming serfdom, servitude, and subjugation. Real freedom is rare. The people of some countries have never known freedom. They do not know what freedom is. They've never tasted it.

The emergence of free-market systems correlates to the emergence of real freedom, and the U.S. is the prime example. Milton Friedman suggested in his book *Capitalism and Freedom* (2002) that the expansion of freedom occurred at the same time development of capitalist and market institutions flourished. Friedman gave an example of how the freedom of capitalism broke the back of tyranny: some of the blacklisted Hollywood writers who invoked the Fifth Amendment when charged with advocating communist overthrow of the government went on selling their scripts under pseudonyms. The scripts were sellable generally as a-political and non-ideological.

Making money for film producers over-rode restraints on the liberty of the writers (who may or may not have been, but some probably were, communist activists). Friedman said that a free economic system acting as a free political system allows advocacy of socialism/communism, but the reverse is not true. A socialist political system will not and cannot tolerate competition from capitalism. This means that for its own survival, socialism will not allow the advocacy of the freedom of capitalism. Under capitalism, free speech or the free effort to make money unshackles the restraints on liberty—restraints that through history are shown to be more common than freedom.

There are some who don't know what they've got in freedom and would naively give it up, even in a relatively small setting. Witness the disastrous saga of the Jim Jones experiment. Much of it happened because of the echoes of Marxism. Recall what befell Jim Jones and his followers:

Jim Jones was an avowed communist. He moved his 900 followers from San Francisco to the jungles of South America where they eventually followed him to their deaths. They drank the poison cool aid. They followed his brand of Marxism to their deaths . . . similar to the Heaven's Gate followers from north San Diego committing suicide on a false promise to meet up with the trailing comet Hale-Bopp.

Safety devices and regulations. Gun owners must lock up their guns. But very soon, technology will recognize the gun-owner handprint so that no one else can fire another's weapon except in an emergency when that protection might be disengaged by the owner.

Regard the gun-owner as a person in charge of a dangerous instrumentality—such as one who cages a wild animal. He should be held to the standards of strict liability. Have him put up a bond or obtain meaningful insurance for payment of compensation should he allow his gun to be stolen, or should he be proven negligent in storing or maintaining the firearm. However in this case, someone would have to come up with a foolproof firewall to prevent the identity of the owner from becoming accessible on a "Hitler's list." More on that below.

Mental competency certifications. Should every gun owner be required to pass a standardized mental competency examination or otherwise prove competency? No, say many, because it is too expensive and takes away our privacy, including medical privacy. Others say that the process of filtering out mentally-dangerous people is too imperfect. Moreover, the process could potentially be abused by a dictator, as happened with the Nazis. Again, there is the issue of being placed on a Hitler's list to consider.

On the other hand, psychologists say there are a few quick tests that could filter out a huge percentage of risky people. Those who test borderline could get more advanced second-stage testing. With the advances now occurring in neuroscience, it soon may take no more than a brain scan to determine whether a person's empathy sites are intact and in good health.

The results of the exams would be subject to review by a truly independent board, and the cost of the testing borne by the gun owner. The right to medical confidentiality, again, must be foolproof. Common ground could be found here for future discoveries and discussion, but the foremost consideration would be to require, again, that a true firewall be created between individuals and a "Hitler's list."

Promote a less-violent culture. Do a better job of reducing violence. Foster less violence in video games, movies, song lyrics, TV shows, arcades, Internet and print media, among others. Do this voluntarily. The government should not mandate such reductions; separate private associations and guilds can develop their own rules.

Do a better job of keeping guns out of the hands of felons and drug dealers. That subject needs little further explanation, except to suggest that anyone knowingly selling, giving, or loaning a gun to such an offender should somehow be answerable to the law.

Family law and domestic relations cases or high passion situations. During separation and divorce, and for a number of years following, or when custody or other high passion-issues are involved, the guns on all sides should be locked up. The lockup should last until special relief is granted by the courts. Many judges include this kind of order in their rulings anyway. During critical times, no-tolerance court orders and injunctions should be in effect

Greater security. Each school district should make its own local decisions regarding security at schools, including whether guards should be hired. Starting up a new government bureaucracy is not necessary or recommended. Former military personal or retired law enforcement officers might earn additional pay to do double duty as a guard as well as perform regularly as teachers, coaches, administrators, or maintenance personnel. Until we can ensure that guns are kept out of the hands of mental patients and terrorists, we recommend that the guarding of children become a part of social existence.

The argument that Fort Hood is an Army base, yet armed guards did not prevent the massacre there, is not persuasive. The Provost Marshal locks up all arms that are not on the firing range or in the hands of base police. The police were guarding the gates, not the medical training facility where the massacre took place. The Provost Marshal specifically disarms medical facilities; thus, the facility was the least-safe place to be once the outer gate was breached. No facility should be left defenseless.

Similarly, the argument that guns should be banned because even the campus police at Virginia Tech could not stop the massacre is also not persuasive. In March of 2012, a jury found Virginia Tech officials negligent, and the families of two of the 33 victims received an award of four million dollars. The other families presumably accepted the offer of settlement. The government levied a hefty fine against the University. The case at this writing is up on appeal.

In Virginia, the biggest problem was that the administrators allegedly covered up the initial shootings for two and a half hours, during which time the shooter continued his rampage. The campus cops, meanwhile, were on a wild goose chase investigating a potential domestic violence issue. Many say that's exactly why we shouldn't have guards. Others say this: if a fire truck takes the wrong road and never shows up at a blaze, does that mean we should abolish fire trucks? So, don't abolish guards.

Thorough background checks on all sales or transfers should be enforced, even at gun shows or between private parties. The problem with this is, again, that anyone on a list is potentially subject to being rounded up by a novo-Hitler. To solve that issue, figure out how to keep a firewall between the list and the government. Perhaps a neutral bonded trustee could maintain the list, subject to inspection by court order and only upon a showing of good cause.

Training certification. Protect against accidents by requiring that all gun owners are certified to handle and store their weapons. Think of it like licensing to drive a car, even though, unlike driving a car, bearing arms is not just a privilege. It is a right—like free speech is.

All registrations, certifications, and backgrounds should be subject to privacy laws. There is always the risk that the government could abuse personal information—as would be the case if Gestapo tactics were adopted to round up all gun owners. There is also the risk of criminals finding out about locations where they might steal guns. The U.S. Supreme Court in Haynes v U.S. (1968) has already held that requiring registration is problematic. Thus, to justify adoption of registrations, a strict privacy law practice should be in place. Firewalls between agencies should be set up.

Any information garnered by the government should be sealed, as medical records or some court records are sealed. Require that a court order to release the information be obtained after showing good cause before information may be accessed by government, law enforcement agencies, or anyone else. Would registration alone have prevented the Sandy Hook tragedy? No; the guns were already registered.

Tax wholesale gun sales. Pay for the protections stated above by setting up a leak-proof fund paid by manufactures and importers, based on volume and the relative value of items per wholesale transaction, e.g. no more than 2%. Or figure out a better way to fund the protections.

Beta testing—unintended consequences. Beware of unintended consequences. We must always be mindful that we might not like what we wished for. So we'd better beta test our solution, or parts of it, before we put it into effect.

So—do you still believe that the 2nd Amendment is merely about letting citizens hunt deer? The clock scale point is presently set at about 2:30. I would try to move it to about 12:45.

A SUGGESTED SOLUTION

To avoid being placed on a "Hitler's list" and to protect the 2d Amendment from further erosion: (1) Privatize the registration list, and (2) adopt the use of Smart Guns.

Gun manufacturers and retail sales outlets would be wise to voluntarily protect themselves from the inevitable class action suit—something the country is inevitably headed for even though the current law saves the gun manufacturers from claims of negligence (Protection of Lawful Commerce in Arms Act was passed by the U.S. Senate on July 29, 2005). I sincerely believe that such act is headed for repeal someday soon. Despite that act, manufacturers and the nation can solve most of the issues dividing the nation on the gun control issue if the manufactures begin insisting that gun buyer's carry liability insurance naming the manufacturer and retailer as co-insured. If such occurs, the insurance carriers should require an ID, address, a background check, a mental competency check, verification of age, citizenship, non-violent felony verification, verification of training and the method of safe-gun storage used. All would be given under oath.

The information then is sealed and held confidential by the insurance carrier; it may not be viewed by the authorities except upon court order after a showing of probable cause. It would be a felony for any person of authority to gain access to this private registration information except through an appropriate court order. The weapon should be verifiable as a smart gun—meaning that it may not be fired by anyone except the registered owner. Such can be accomplished by any number of means: e.g. an electronic device that would read a fingerprint, or an iris of the eye, etc. or even a mechanized code known only to the owner.

12

Economics and Political Systems

A comedian's viewpoint: How do you know that the American people are headed for more financial trouble? Answer: CEO's, the Congress, and hookers are merging so they can screw the American people more efficiently!

The quintessential economic system is efficient: peak production per man hour equals the greatest quantity and quality achievable at the lowest cost and with the least waste of energy, time, and resources. In this system, the worker earns a reasonable wage, is free—that is, is not part of a totalitarian society—is appreciated, and appreciates his employer. He has friends, loved ones, belongs to a group, and his environment is preserved. Most significantly, the market is free and competitive, yet the important characteristic of self-interest is by nature synthesized with intuitive ethics and morality.

We're talking about rational self-interest here. Even Ayn Rand qualified her definition of "self-interest" with the adjective *rational*. Through the ages, the entrepreneurs' plight has been to decide fundamental economic questions: what will be produced, how will it be produced, and who will own the resources of productivity? There is no doubt that man's competitive drive for production, trade, and distribution has been in existence for a long time. Ultimately, however, there perhaps is no true *pure* competition. Otherwise, no one could ever make the money necessary to accumulate capital.

What does that mean? It means that pure competition between entities would eat up all the wished-for left-over profits. But in actuality the elements work together and the result—nature's result—is a sum greater than the whole of its parts, as in synergism. Under that phenomenon a good operator would have some profits left over even after heavy competition.

Perhaps the main reason for this synergism or this phenomenon is that ultimately imperfections and niches abound in the free market system. The imperfections and niches are from the chaos that is natural in the co-opetition equation. These niches or market pools also may be developed in many other ways, including via networking, trade-offs of mutual benefit, sharing, referrals, advertising, patents, proprietary rights, price and cost cutting, and degrees of inefficiency or x-efficiency.

However, in cases where niches grow into oversized caverns and draw in excessive shares of the market, they have the propensity to become gaping monopolies. For a period of time, they may restrict competition and balloon into even bigger monopolies. We all recall, for example, the story of Standard Oil Company, founded by John D. Rockefeller, who became the richest man in the world.

Anti-monopoly (anti-trust) laws were enacted near the turn of the century—1900. The U.S. Supreme Court broke up Standard Oil in 1911. Thirty-three separate companies were created from the break up.

Monopoly can also occur if the niches are created through bribery, crime, price-fixing, or illegitimate governmental influence—that is, by breaking the intuitive or codified rules of co-opetition. In the past, monopolies tended to flourish in the free-market system to the detriment of the very free-market system that generated them. Obviously, this is a matter of degree. In the grossest cases, to correct imbalance and preserve free enterprise, as said above, society asked the government to step in with antitrust laws to reign back monopolies. In this way cooperation (and forced cooperation) came into play to offset overly aggressive monopolistic competition (as reflected by the policies of President Theodore Roosevelt in about 1890–1900). Even Rome tried to curb monopolies, with varying degrees of success.

Many argue that given enough time, smaller, more efficient companies will rise up and out-compete monopolies. This is the strong plank of many Libertarians. In reality, this is a problematic prospect. By using political influence and other questionable means for maintaining the position of his business, the monopolist actually has a huge arsenal of weapons at its disposal. For example, if the monopoly controls all the raw materials necessary for the manufacture of its products—a vertical monopoly—no outsider could successfully compete with it.

THE MARXIST CASE

Socialists and/or Communists reject not only the idea that the free market can achieve an equitable and efficient system, but reject private ownership of capital entirely. Karl Marx wrote his thesis during a time when he believed that the free market was hardly "free" due to the existence of massive monopolies. His theme was that there was an impoverished working class, and ownership of resources lay with a scarce few.

At times of economic crisis, he claimed, some people starved, and conditions for human life became appalling. He did not like the industrial revolution. He wanted to regress to the old shop-keeper system of money-changers, guilds, and apprenticeships. He believed that because populations were moving to the cities, in many respects, the family was becoming obsolete. Marx's famous quote, "From each according to his abilities, to each according to his needs" is the epitome of a cooperative system.

In principle, it seems to be an enormously appealing idea from the perspective of the masses. In reality, it is inherently and fatally flawed. It is fatally flawed primarily because it wastefully redistributes money (spends it) rather than puts it back to work building more capital (invests it); and it attempts to totally manage a system—the economic system—too complex for mankind to operate without the aid of mother nature.

Because of socialism's inherent forced-cooperation imbalance of the co-opetition equation, a socialist utopia or even a true socialistic economic endeavor has never been successfully achieved, and never will be. It is a deception and an illusion. Such systems deny the beneficial competition counterbalance to forced cooperation; they do not utilize the competitive nature of humankind that we observe again and again. Under unchecked socialism, the government itself inevitably becomes *the* giant monopoly. Without competition, inefficiency reigns, bureaucracy burgeons, and the system fails. It fails every time.

Again, a big reason it fails is that any significant attempt to manage a complex system like an economy, without leaving room for nature to work her magic, will bog down in inefficiency. Allowed to do her work, nature simplifies and helps in the management and operation of any complex system.

What does "nature" mean in this context? Mainly, it means the proper application of the "competition" part of "co-opetition." Nature *intuitively generally seeks* the ultimate synthesis. Nature is the primal wisdom I wish you to see and recognize.

Closet Communists—they are the true socialists—doggedly refuse to realize the degree of self-destruction they have wrought and will continue to wreak on themselves and all who naively follow them. They don't leave room for nature to work her magic. In *Doctor Zhigavo*, Boris Pasternak dramatized how the Red commander finally woke up to what was happening. He had knocked himself to pieces for the cause, believing that the ends justified the means, only to find that it led to empty dreams.

The Russian Revolution was commandeered by the Marxist Bolsheviks from a provisional government a little after the strife had spontaneously ignited through a leaderless, populist uprising. Soon after the Czar was overthrown, the Bolsheviks, also known as the Red Russians, defeated the White Russians—generally the non-socialists. Later, the Bolsheviks officially changed their name, but not their philosophy, to Communists/ Communism.

Millions of people were forced into gulags in Siberia, killed outright, or died of hunger or cold during the needlessly mob-extended revolution. The revolution's motto—the "ends justifies the means"—led to purges and the pointless deaths of more millions of people.

Marx could not have foreseen that the free-enterprise Industrial Revolution would create a vast middle class. That development of the middle class not only resulted in raising the standard of living of the "proletariat," but in the Western capitalistic system, it blurred the distinction between the bourgeoisie and the lower class.

Marx also could not have foreseen that the bourgeoisie would come to realize that the standard of living of the proletariat must be raised enough for the proletariat to afford to buy capitalist/ bourgeoisie-produced goods—cars, refrigerators, houses, television sets. He could not have foreseen that proletariat trade-union pension funds, for example, would end up owning a vast proportion of the stock of the bourgeoisie's companies. He could not see that each faction would see that they needed to synthesize their differences in order for both factions to prosper. He could not see that free market and the workings of Mother Nature, aka Adam Smith's Invisible Hand, and her magic would accomplish perhaps ninety percent of the *synthesis*, and do it for free.

AFFORDING A MODEL T

Most of us know the philosophy of Henry Ford when he was selling his Model T car: He paid his employees enough so they could afford to buy the Model T themselves. This is strong evidence of the folly of Marx's reasoning. His idea that modern industrialists all followed a course leading to exploitation of the proletariat is wrong. Business and free enterprise, or capitalism, is not so-called Darwinian competition: it is overwhelmingly co-opetition.

The free market is the oxygen of human life. It is primal wisdom. With free enterprise intuitively driving the marketplace and guiding national and international governance, the economies of the world will truly flourish. Ford cooperated with his workers by paying them well enough that they could afford to buy his cars. Thus, he more successfully competed in the auto industry. That is what I call co-opetition.

For centuries, humankind has been almost obsessed with the quest for Utopia. Many thought Marxism was the answer. But even Fidel Castro admitted in the summer of 2010 that Marxism does not work (see "Fidel Latest to Say Cuba's Communism Doesn't Work," Paul Haven, *Associated Press*, September 9, 2010). Throughout the world during the twentieth century, the unintended consequences of the experiment of Marxism were nothing short of catastrophic. And they still are.

We have seen example after example of failure. Look at South Korea, with one of the leading economies in the word compared to North Korea, with probably the worst; or West Berlin compared to East Berlin during the Cold War. Compare the United States at the time the Berlin Wall fell, which was then by far and still is—despite our current problems—the number one economy in the world, to the collapsed Soviet Union.

Compare socialist Cuba and Venezuela to the successful capitalist nations Chili and Peru. Compare the big government-leaning U.S. states like left-leaning California and New York, both rushing into insolvency while conservative Texas, Utah and, among others, recently turned-around Ohio, Indiana and Wisconsin are doing well—in the latter cases thanks to Governors' John Kasich, Ohio; Mike Pense, present, and Mitch Daniels, past, of Indiana and Scott Walker, of Wisconsin respectively. (Also, see "The Best States for Business," Kurt Badenhousen, *Forbes.com*, October 13, 2010). In Wisconsin's case, the wonderful reform and turnaround accomplished by conservative Governor Scott Walker is truly startling . . .

Compare the monstrous suffering of Maoist China with the emerging capitalist-leaning China. Canada, left-leaning in 1995, had a debt problem proportionally about as bad as that of the U.S. at the date of this writing. Yet beginning in the late 1990s,

Canada cut its governmental spending—against the social-ist-leaning grain—and eventually balanced its budget. In 2013, it led the U.S. by far in the ratio of debt to gross national product. The Canadian economy booms while the U.S. economy, at this writing still limps, except for the inflation and Fed-driven stock market. ("Lessons from the Great White North," Nita Ghei, *Washington Times,* June 11, 2011).

Journalists: I pray you will give these comparisons a fair assessment. Shake free of the undue influence of the still-lingering echoes of Marxism of the last century. As I will demonstrate, redistribution is not finance. It is a form of raiding—what the cave man regularly did to other tribes before he discovered the benefits of trading. Redistribution is contrary to logic; it is contrary to nature. More than ever, our nation needs to hear your unbiased voice and your objective ruminations and commentary.

A thought to ponder: Did the teachings of Marx and his Bolshevik followers have anything to do with to the unintended consequence of Hitler's maniacal acts of genocide? Hitler was a socialist ("Nazi" is an acronym for National Socialist). The Bolsheviks were socialists. However, the Marxist/Bolshevik brand of socialism knew no borders. It was meant to be *world* socialism. On the other hand, socialist Hitler believed in uniting the German-speaking people within national borders. He rejected Bolshevik socialism as unpatriotic to Germany.

In 1917, after the Bolsheviks took over the Russian peoples, a young, paranoid Hitler worried about them taking over Germany in the same way—and in fact, Marxists did gain substantial control of Germany for a period of two or three years after World War I. Both Hitler and Joseph Stalin, who'd become the genocidal dictator of the Soviet Union, labored under their respective interpretations of the unproven, illogical ideal of socialism.

History demonstrates that socialism in the hands of these exponents inevitably led to the Second World War and the Soviet Gulags (*The Gulag Archipelago*, by Aleksandr Solzhenitsyn) and finally the collapse of the Soviet Union. None of these totalitarian leaders could fathom that within free enterprise and capitalism, the trait of co-opetition is necessarily, and by nature, generated as a byproduct of good business commerce. They believed, along with Fascist/socialist Mussolini, that economies—whether worldwide or national—could be, and should be, managed—and manage theirs they did, with heavy-handed governmental regulation.

Experience and history have proved that economies are too complex to be managed in that way. They are like the giant mobile from Chapter 3, where you touch one hanging piece and you have no idea which other pieces will move or in what direction.

As much as possible, let the market manage itself naturally through the workings of co-opetition. Let mother nature work her magic. Yes, correct white-collar crime and abuse, but first by exercising the common law that originated with Rome and Phoenicia—And, only then, if absolutely necessary, do it by a minimum of sensible regulations. Only with great wisdom and caution should the hand of man attempt to adjust the fulcrum on the sliding scale of co-opetition. There can and should be debate as to precisely where that point is, but just knowing of the concept of *the synthesis* will give critical guidance.

The primary objectives of spending on social services should be for crime prevention, fire, ambulance, basic local education, health, Social Security and basic social safety-nets, certain public transportation and roads, bridges and dams, parks, a modicum of apolitical arts, border and military protection. Social engineering should be attempted only with caution. Manipulation of the free market as part of a social engineering experiment runs the risk of unforeseen consequences—movement of an unknown piece of the giant mobile. For example, subprime mortgage [social engineering] triggered the Great Recession of 2008 according to economist and Fed Chair Alan Greenspan.

That is not to say that all social engineering is inherently bad. As mentioned above, most people would accept a safety-net for the truly needy but not a hammock. First, however, run experiments on the rare, deserving, and well-thought out programs. Find and iron out the wrinkles before subjecting the nation to massive unintended consequences. In the U.S. we have fifty states, not to mention the territories, from which to pick spots for experimentation.

SOCIAL SECURITY—A FORM OF SOCIAL ENGINEERING. IT'S PURPOSE: GOOD—A SAFETY NET. IT'S METHOD: NEEDS HELP.

We already have great experience with Social Security—and yes, it is a form of social engineering. But it is valuable and necessary. Still, it needs some tweaking. The system is going broke. It was never properly financed; our leaders got off on the wrong foot in the 1930s. At present, Congress routinely raids the fund in a giant Ponzi scheme. Now that we know more, we can do Social Security the right way.

You see, SS in substance was based on *redistribution*, not capitalism. It deducts money—payroll taxes—from workers and gives it to retired people. It does not make a good faith effort to first put the money to work to earn and build capital—earnings that can be later used to pay retirees. It doesn't properly invest the fund as would a capitalist; for the most part, it simply disburses it, raids it, and redistributes it.

The most logical current thinking is that the funds should be invested and, to the greatest extent possible, deposited with a true trustee or with fiduciaries for management. That way the fund would be operated as a true trusteeship and invested in the safest of securities, such as gold, U.S. treasury bonds, or blue chips. Since the biggest foreign countries in the world have the confidence to invest in U.S. debt, why not us?

However, all potential conflicts of interest must be eliminated from the trusteeship. You can't have the government's hand too close to the cookie jar. Congress and the Presidents' have been raiding- "borrowing"- from the fund for other projects and have not put the money back. If the government tried to replace it with a proper interest return today, it would go broke trying.

The ideal is that any worthy social-engineering program should, whenever possible, pay for itself and be undertaken only after long, hard study and under strict conditions. I reiterate, if we need to experiment, let's first do it in an arena outside the federal government. Experiment in one of the states or territories.

Or on the other hand, Social Security could take the form of free-market investment where the fund earns its way and pays for itself—where the workings of nature simplify the system. Which method is better, redistribution or investment?

The Marxist phrase "From each according to his abilities, to each according to his needs" is pure unadulterated redistribution; it does not pay for itself. It is illogical nonsense. To enable the economy to flourish where the rising tide lifts all ships— including the raft of the impoverished—the incentive of profit for risk-takers must exist. Otherwise, why take the risk at all? Too little return for the risk-taker means we kill the goose that lays the golden egg. Based on my experience in the business world and corporate law, it can take a return as high as from 15 to

28 percent or more per year to entice a risk-taker to invest! It's called an *internal rate of return* or cash on cash return.

An obvious purpose of this work is to debunk myths surrounding Socialism, and get the insidious seeds of Marxism out of our brains . . . get rid of the idea of redistribution, and utilize the magical free workings of nature, capitalism, and the free market.

The "Wall Street Protesters" and certain political ideologists make reference to social Darwinism as a negative reality of capitalism. No, they are confused. When one group raids the resources of another group—as does redistribution—that is social Darwinism. As we said, *raiding* was the preferred method of gaining resources of the prehistoric tribes. Then they evolved naturally to prefer *trading*. Yes, they found it better to trade, than to raid. Capitalism is the epitome of trading. Redistribution is the epitome of raiding. No successful business or economy on earth has ever been based on redistribution, so why are they still trying to force it down our throats?

Killing the goose that laid the golden egg has occurred in every country that adopted Marxist ideas. China has partially learned this lesson now. In international trade and business, she ironically veils her Communism while moving very much into capitalism—and *the synthesis*. But China is still subject to the Law of Unintended Consequences: as of 2013, she is a country favoring her own government-operated businesses and raising the bar on private and foreign investment and innovation. In other words, she continues to avoid offering foreigners a fair playing field in the national Chinese market.

As of 2013, China has lost at least two large cases before the World Trade Organization—one for imposing excessive duties on U.S. exports of chickens, the other for over-subsidizing her auto industry. (*The Business Journals*, "Hey China, don't play chicken with U.S.," Kent Hoover, Aug., 2, 2013). In that regard, she at least sometimes cooperates even as she competes; she does, after all, submit to the WTO. But if she continues subsidizing her own businesses, especially the government-operated ones, she will soon hit the wall—too much forced cooperation, and not enough free-enterprise—i.e., competition. If China experiments with social engineering without being aware of the unintended consequences, and merely guesses at environmental corrections (or the lack of them), she could very well squander all her recent gains.

Sean, an acquaintance currently doing business in China, described his own perspective. The Chinese economy will hit the wall, he said, for two main reasons, both of them examples of the violation of the *ultimate synthesis*. China is over-subsidizing its own companies to the disadvantage of competitors from off its shores, and it is seriously manipulating its currency.

These interferences in the free market could lead to dependence on the government by the locals. Also, Sean stated, some Chinese companies have been weak on ethics in their offshore business dealings. Perhaps because his business was relatively small, he had great difficulty maintaining quality control. He had problems with credibility. These are examples of failure of Adam Smith's workings of the Invisible Hand. If businessmen cannot trust each other, business grinds to a halt. Effective January 2011, Sean pulled his operations out of China.

Because it is good business to leave a little something on the table so people can afford to buy goods, the built-in cooperation (the Invisible Hand) that allows *the synthesis* to work exists inherently in capitalism. The Chinese must have intuitively rediscovered this natural co-opetition, at least from the standpoint of the locals—but they appear to have a long way to go regarding international business.

THE OTHER EXTREME

The other side of the spectrum of economic systems is, of course, the conservative extreme. A Libertarian would charge that the government should provide only minimal services for its people. True Libertarians say that the government should stay out of most forms of services. Some even go so far as to say "no" to anti-monopoly laws and "yes" to legalizing marijuana. Except for basic needs, they say "no" to socially engineered health and safety regulations, "no" to immigration restrictions, and "no" to any other governmental program except for police, fire, emergency, disease contagion control, and civil defense. Essentially, to the Libertarian no governmental intervention should take place. They believe that it destroys the efficient mechanisms of the free market and is, furthermore, the cause of many distortions, including the formation of monopolies.

On the other hand, the mainstream conservative believes that Social Security, workers' safety laws, zoning regulations, health codes, basic environmental laws, local or state minimum education standards, and some well-conceived and tested state or local social engineering services are acceptable. Those that result from pressure by the people through legislative processes are generally aimed at counterbalancing and trimming the parts of totally free competition that hang over the edge into the category of excessive competition. The forms of excessive competition referred to here—fraud, white-collar crime, cartels, and price fixing—against which such controls are directed, are also manifestations of selfish egoism.

How can sensible Libertarians justify the inherent inconsistency and irreconcilable ideologies of their theory? The answer is co-opetition, the *ultimate synthesis*. The conflicted Libertarian can reconcile his *exceptions to the rules* of Libertarianism by recognizing that, perhaps, he is actually an intuitive co-opetitionist. He could then merely shift the fulcrum and find the sweet spot of the tug of war between cooperation and competition for any particular issue.

The degree upon which cooperation should be imposed, therefore, is the question. Throughout this analysis, a distinction must remain constantly in mind: lobbying in support of special interest groups as a means of protecting or expanding niches is a form of competition, while governmental regulation to promote group benefit imposed against the general freedom of individuals is a form of cooperation.

Control of monopolies, cartels, and price fixers adopted first at the turn of the twentieth century up through the 1930s in the United States, have provided a great safety valve. Such interventions perhaps saved the country from a naïve, reactionary rush in the direction of socialism and Communism. Thus, the control of business/ corporate monopolies, like touching parts of the giant mobile, indirectly served to slow the then-seemingly inevitable creep of Communism and massive government bureaucratic monopolies—bureaucracies that breed and flourish as a concomitant element of socialism.

Anti-monopoly and antitrust laws gave individuals a right of private action, in some cases treble damages, as a disincentive to would-be monopolists. In the 1930s, the Libertarian view of "hands-off " was not followed, and the cooperative governmental control of monopolies helped stem a reactionary movement toward Communism and socialism.

SELF-INTEREST VERSUS GROUP INTEREST

Some years ago, in their book *The Seven Cultures of Capitalism,* Hampden-Turner and Trompenaars showed that seven of the large Western European industrial nations (Germany, France, Italy, England, Spain, Switzerland, Holland) and Canada and the U.S. plus Japan, embrace some form of competitive/cooperative economic system—that is, in my view, the beginnings of co-opetitive systems. However, there is little evidence that anyone consciously understood or was even cognizant of the principles of co-opetition.

Most likely, after World War II some of these cultures arrived at their respective systems as if the workings of Adam Smith's Invisible Hand were in play. This occurred when some of those systems were opened to free enterprise, and others maintained their free enterprises even in the face of socialist-leaning populations. Even the post–World War II economic and political systems of Germany and Japan, which were originally the products of planning, in the aftermath of the war were constantly engaged in internal struggle between the influences of Socialism verses Capitalism.

With increasing education, wisdom, and experience in the field of economics, the necessity of synthesis became, and will become, more obvious. The Invisible Hand element of capitalism did and will gradually inject a form of self-executing co-opetition into these systems. "Self-executing co-opetition" in short, means that nature, intuition, and the workings of the free-market (as opposed primarily to government-forced cooperation) will point to the best economic fulcrum position for each country.

This situation varies considerably among the above-mentioned seven Western cultures. The long and unique cultures and traditions of the people of each nation are major factors for determining the relative co-opetitive balance in each system.

In my view, some of these systems would not work well if adopted by cultures other than their own. Although I agree with and champion the idea of synthesizing the forces of self-interest verses group-interest, some teachings of *The Seven Cultures of Capitalism* lean heavily toward cooperation. In the area of employee relations, for example, the book argues that if a bonus for good work is given only to a singled-out individual, other workers would tend to resent that person and, therefore, the company, too. This results in less overall productivity. The book holds that a better practice would be to reward, instead, the worker team rather than the outstanding individual.

In my view, the emphasis should be quite different. If the individual is not separately rewarded, he would be more inclined to lose motivation, especially if the others freeload off the efforts of the achieving worker. Although I recognize that seldom does anyone make it totally alone, a better method is to institute what I refer to as "self-executing co-opetition balancing." Again, this means to put the workers into an archetypal win/win or beneficial self-interest situation. Give a proportionally bigger bonus to the inventive-achiever worker, but at the same time give a smaller general bonus to his team or group.

By this method, the self-interest incentive keeps the achiever happy and working, yet keeps the others working with him to achieve potential secondary bonuses for themselves as well. This scenario would result in fewer malingerers freeloading off the achiever and less reason for the achiever to lose incentive.

In *The Tortoise Shell Game*, Andrea passionately moves to free her dad, Anthony, not only because she adores him, but also because it will clear the family name from stigma that could unjustly jeopardize her fiancé Rich's professional career. A synthesis of empathy for him and her self-interest.

MACROECONOMICS AND GOVERNMENTAL ROLE

The first part of this section concerns the issue of whether or not governmental control is warranted, and if so, to what extent. Monetary and fiscal policies and the application of *the synthesis* are discussed. "Monetary policy" refers to tightening or loosening the supply of funds. "Fiscal policy" refers to increasing or lowering tax rates and expenditures. Both are forms of governmental (or government-sanctioned) control— evidence of cooperation or forced-cooperation as defined in this work.

Upon careful consideration, I am convinced that some such control or regulation is necessary for maintenance of the asymmetric balance of *the synthesis*. But very often, even a little too much governmental control, like one more pinch of salt, can ruin the soup.

Foremost in our thoughts should always be the potential for unintended consequences. When monetary and fiscal controls or regulations overbalance free-market forces, the general economy becomes subject to exaggerated swings. As has occurred in the past, such perturbations can lead, for example, to catastrophes like the Great Depression of the early 1930s, the runaway inflation and horrendous interest rates of the Jimmy Carter presidency, and the Great Recession of 2008 and beyond.

Remember the analogy of the outrigger canoe depicted on the cover of this book as it relates to a well-working economy. In the main hull symbolically resides competition in the form of free-enterprise, individualism, freedom, a bit of chaos, and risk. However, cooperation symbolically resides in the out-rigged pontoon in the form of regulation, law, and order. Together, they are an asymmetric balance, with the fulcrum and much greater weight near the main hull. The outrigged pontoon should be only as large as is necessary to keep the canoe from capsizing in a storm—keep the economy from capsizing, but not so large that it might slow the canoe, which symbolizes the economy, down.

A MISGUIDED SOCIAL-ENGINEERING EXPERIMENT

As we discussed earlier, our clearest present-day example of unintended consequences was the sub-prime mortgage, Freddie Mac and Fannie Mae collapse of 2008; this fiasco grew primarily from an attempt by Congress—commenced under Jimmy Carter, boosted under Bill Clinton and continued under G. W. Bush—to socially engineer home ownership for millions of American buyers who could not otherwise qualify for home loans. The condition was exacerbated by Wall Street greed and fraud. As seen in 2009, such government-led over-cooperation effectively triggered the near destruction of the U.S. and world economies.

All these consequences were unintended and a result of unwise governmental interference in the free market: that is, over-cooperation. No synthesis, no asymmetric balance. Clearly, we did not learn our lessons from the Great Depression of the 1930s.

GOVERNMENT MEDDLING PROLONGS
GREAT DEPRESSION

Many leading economists argue that the U.S. languished in the Depression of the 1930s for an extra ten years largely because of governmental policies restricting competition, i.e. the outrigger canoe's pontoon was too fat.

In those post-Depression years, government labor laws protected Big Labor so that wages remained artificially high. That is, they did not drop commensurate with the over-supply of labor during the Depression-era market. The result was that vastly fewer people could get jobs; those who got them received relatively high benefits and were generally overpaid for the depressed labor marketplace and the times. A truly free-labor market would have put wages at a lower level—a free market level—leaving room for more workers to get jobs.

Other economists assert that the main reason the Depression lasted so long was because of increased tariffs dictated by government and the manipulation of monetary policies by the Federal Reserve, compounded by Roosevelt's ill-conceived fiscal policy of raising taxes during a depression. Either way, the main culprit responsible for the slow recovery was clearly interference in the free market. It was an example of over-cooperation and inadequate *synthesis*.

Some economic historians assert that during the 1920s, when the tax rate for the wealthy was lowered from over 70 percent to no higher than 25 percent, capital was reinvested and the economy roared. But under President Hoover and then Roosevelt, when taxes of the wealthy were raised to over 75 percent (and eventually much higher), the economy choked, capital was not reinvested, and the Great Depression continued for almost ten years (see "The Great Depression: Myths and Facts," Don Boudreaux, *Forbes.com*, May 5, 2009).

So, contrary to Hollywood's naive and insipid interpretation of *The Great Gatsby* by F. Scott Fitzgerald, the Great Depression was not caused by the Roaring Twenties and its supposed excesses. It was caused by a confluence of later factors, including inept manipulation by the Federal Reserve, compounded by the actions of raising taxes and raising trade barriers, and the fact that salaries of many people were kept artificially high, prolonging unemployment. I see it as another failure resulting from unknowing misapplication of co-opetition—the failure to find the sweet spot.

A full gold standard-commodities monetary system is on the free-market competition side of the scale (the Scylla advocates, according to Nobel Prize-winning economist Milton Friedman). To install a regulatory element to it, such as the Federal Reserve to manage it (the Charybodis advocates), adds some cooperation (acquiesced or forced) to the equation. So far, such is a recipe for finding the proper synthesis, the sweet spot, between the two.

But too much of one side of the scale or too much of the other doesn't work. It can be a recipe for failure for not properly exercising the regulation, or for not finding *the synthesis*. Not finding the synthesis is exactly what happened when, in the opinion of Friedman, the Federal Reserve did not pump liquidity into the banking system quickly enough at the beginning of the Depression.

Because of that failure, suggests Friedman, the world economy and America's economy would have been better off without the Federal Reserve. But a properly operated Federal reserve would be best of all; it could more readily have achieved *the synthesis*. I believe that if the Fed members had been aware of the principle of co-opetition they would have acted more nimbly.

UNPREDICTABLE GOVERNMENTAL POLICIES

Under the Carter administration during the 1970s, the U.S. economy struggled with a spike of interest to 22 percent and runaway inflation. This occurred in large part because of unpredictable governmental policies, government overspending, the oil crisis, and a wage/price spiral. Carter should have cut spending, adopted less big labor-friendly policies, and pushed for higher domestic oil production.

Later, the country suffered multibillions of dollars of losses during the collapse of the savings and loan and real estate industries, thanks in large degree to the abruptness of the tax changes enacted during the Reagan administration in 1986, including an abrupt elimination of certain real estate tax shelters compounded by relaxation of rules against conflict of interest-investing by the S&Ls. Since a major part of my law practice at that time involved real estate developments as well as representing two or three Savings and Loan associations, I saw the disaster coming. I predicted the result to my colleagues.

Congress enacted 26 U.S.C. § 469, which related to limitations on deductions for passive activity losses and limitations on passive activity credits. The new law removed many tax shelters, especially for real estate investments, and significantly decreased the value of many such investments. This contributed to the end of the real estate boom of the early- to mid-1980s and facilitated the savings and loan crisis. Of the 3,234 savings and loan associations in the United States at the time, 747 failed. Some $402 billion was lost, at an estimated additional cost of $370 billion.

This occurred primarily because of the unwise method of legislative interference in the free market. The changes were not adequately eased into effect—no proper synthesis, no foresight. Over-cooperation regarding tax shelters, and over-competition, regarding deregulation contributed to destabilization. Both the pontoon and the main hull became too fat.

The legislature rationalized its easing of protections against conflicts of interest under the guise of "deregulation." Everyone wants to reduce regulation, but conflicts of interest should never be deregulated away. You never let the fox stand guard in the chicken coop, which is why rules against conflicts of interest have been with us since before Rome and Phoenicia.

All this was compounded by the bureaucratic ineptitude of the Federal Home Loan Bank Board and the Federal Resolution Trust Corporation. (As an attorney, I had first-hand experience with it. I broke free $12,000,000 from the grips of that government agency in the Federal District Court separation of powers case of *Tucker v Home Federal*).

The unintended consequences of the '86 tax change by Congress, commenced during the Reagan administration, had it's impact during that of George H. W. Bush.

ILL-CONCEIVED SOCIAL-ENGINEERING
ALSO CAUSED GREAT RECESSION OF 2008

As I have said, judging by the far lower number of people now working in this country, we're still suffering through the Great Recession of 2008, the worst since the Great Depression of the last century. Former Federal Reserve Chairman Alan Greenspan testified before Congress that the subprime mortgage bubble was the main culprit that triggered this recession (see "Greenspan Testifies to Financial Crises Commission, Blames Fannie and Freddie," Ryan McCarthy, Huffington Post, April 7, 2010).

It is important to detail what we touched on in the opening chapters: social engineering programs enacted by Congress and advocated or acquiesced-to by three Presidents of the U.S. were directly responsible for the subprime mortgage bubble. Again, interference in the workings of the free market—excessive cooperation—nearly destroyed not only the U.S. economy, but almost the entire economy of the world as well.

To restate: during his term, President Bill Clinton amended the Community Reinvestment Act, which gave home mortgages to borrowers who could not afford them. That social engineering program "guaranteed" (implicitly and effectively) most of the paper securing the home loans made to low-to-moderate-income buyers through the quasi-governmental agencies of Freddie Mac and Fannie Mae.

According to the book, *Reckless Endangerment* (below), in about 2008, it came to light that the administrators of those agencies had left them hundreds of billions in the hole. No one had properly exercised control over the agencies. Congressman Barney Frank and other Democrats including Senator Chris Dodd had led Congressional social engineers in the continuing mistaken implementation of that debacle. (see *Reckles$ Endangerment*, Gretchen Morgenson and Joshua Rosner, 2011).

When G. W. Bush and the Republican Congress belatedly tried to audit those agencies in 2004-2005, the Democrat-controlled Senate blocked it. An audit might have headed off the crises, for just three years later the subprime mortgage bubble burst, triggering the 2008 crash of the economy.

Although their goal seemed noble—that every one should be able to own a home-the method they employed lacked both common sense and knowledge of the workings of the free market and of *the synthesis.*

The agencies of Freddie Mac and Fannie Mae, having "guaranteed" securities, which would otherwise have been very high risk, now had to get rid of the bad paper they were stuck with. Of course, lenders and loan brokers made serious money from such financing and were not unhappy making those fees.

When the bubble burst, and Freddie Mac and Fannie Mae went insolvent, the problems escalated into the economic crash of the entire world. The fact that Wall Street devised instruments intended to re-package and hide the toxic loans certainly compounded the disaster. But that was primarily a bad *effect;* the subprime social engineering was the cause of the crash. The windfall money the brokers made off it was not the original intent; that was an unintended consequence. Again, this is an example of government over-cooperation, which Wall Street then whipsawed into over-competition by packaging and selling bad securities.

The effect was fraud by some in Wall Street—fraud in wrapping the resultant bad (mortgage) paper into the disguise of credit default swap (stock securities) paper in order to help the guarantors of the bad paper rid themselves of it. There was no synthesis. No co-opetition.

UNTESTED EXPERIMENTATION WITH SOCIAL-ENGINEERING IS DANGEROUS

It seems logical that tested law to counter white-collar crime is less dangerous to an economy than are untested social-engineering laws where unintended consequences can be catastrophic. Perhaps such social-engineering programs should be left primarily in the purview of the individual states, which could act as testing grounds, before the entire nation adopts the program?

When we assess the extent to which the government *should* interfere with the workings of Adam Smith's Invisible Hand, we must recognize that morality and ethics, as I've said before, are inherently part of capitalism. Otherwise, the system would never have evolved; very little trade and business would have ever gotten done.

Ethics arise naturally, or intuitively, as a cooperative aspect of the ultimate synthesis. The Invisible Hand that enables the economy to work is in operation naturally. Cultivate it. Let it do its job. Don't break it off at the wrist and stuff it down the throat of the economy. Don't choke off thriving economies like what happened at the end of the roaring 20s.

For a species to survive, an animal must possess some ego-ism—a strong urge to secure food and to defend its means of earning a livelihood. For humans this impulse is, of course, the driving competitive force of an economy. The human animal extends egoism from the individual to his family while he fights for the interests of his mate and his young. He will even fight for his town and his country.

On closer examination, we see that the individual also has an instinctive need to belong to a team for survival. Thus, social life is of also great importance, and the pursuit of self-interest is mitigated by respect and compassion for others. So when I refer to self-interest, I'm talking about *rational* self-interest, *moral* self-interest, or *ordered* self-interest.

In prehistoric times, a society of unmitigated egoists would have knocked itself to pieces. On the other hand, a society with perfectly altruistic individuals would have soon starved. Human instincts have not changed, so there seems to be a conflict between contrary tendencies, each of which is necessary for exis-tence. We need a set of rules by which to reconcile them.

These rules, for the most part, are already available by view-ing the workings of nature. However, because of our speedy rise to modernism and the unwitting distortion of these inherited injunctions, we must now put mechanisms into play so that overly competitive individuals have to adhere to the rules, even when those rules interfere with their immediate advantage. Although humans have a natural instinct to synthesize social and egotistic demands into co-opetition, in many cases there is also a reason to set the co-opetitive parameters by law.

THE INVISIBLE HAND REVEALED

Let us refer back to the teachings of Adam Smith—his philosophy, rather than *Wealth of Nations*. In true capitalism, there is a natural tendency and need to temper self-interest with a sense of benevolence and community. For most people this is accomplished through intuition and culture or tradition. For those on the fringes, however, some carefully designed, light-handed governmental regulation (cooperation, forced or acquiesced) becomes necessary, mainly to control white-collar crime.

As was said earlier, Adam Smith spoke of free enterprise, or simply "enterprise," when describing a natural system that contains within it the workings of the market as if guided by an "Invisible Hand." Using other words, co-opetition is what he described. From an economics standpoint, I believe that the concepts of this *synthesis* and free enterprise are, in fact, synonymous.

As we said, by necessity free enterprise is both competitive and cooperative. For enterprise to prosper and endure, businesspeople must deal with one another ethically and in good faith. They must cooperate according to the customary rules and practices of their field, subject to common business law, and they must trade in good faith and trust. Otherwise business would grind to a halt and chaos and raiding would ensue.

Recall the 1987 film Wall Street 1, starring Michel Douglas (who received the Academy Award for it) with Charlie and Martin Sheen and Daryl Hannah, directed and co-written by Oliver Stone. Michael Douglas's character declares in a speech that "greed is good."

The idea that dog-eat-dog business practices are a good thing, or that "greed is good," is simply wrong. We all know that the Invisible Hand of business ethics is what enables free enterprise to flourish. Even as businesspeople compete for the highest price or greatest market share, they must also cooperate. It is as though business people force themselves, either consciously or non-consciously, to deal with each other (for the most part) in a fair and trustworthy manner for the benefit of all—and to enable the market to work.

This is why peoples of disparate backgrounds, languages, and political structures, even in ancient times, have been able to trade with each other, transporting and exchanging all around the globe, spices, salt, beads and shells, gold, gems, silk, and other commodities. The advancement of mercantilism would not have occurred unless cooperation was a crucial part of doing business.

The raiders and parasites who seek advantage in business transactions by preying on the reasonable expectations of good faith business people and consumers are not being co-opetitive. They are competitive to a fault, and therefore disrupt the synthesis of co-opetition.

Dating back to Roman times and that of the mercantilist Phoenicians, the common law has generally corrected such overly-competitive, "greedy" entities. For example, it is clearly wrong for people in a fiduciary position or a trusteeship to suffer a conflict of interest in their relationships. Yet incredibly, and contrary to common law, modern governments have been known to exempt elements of the business world from such proscriptions.

They do so under the misguided idea that allowing a little necessary evil into the balance will foster smoother trading. (See "Conflict of Interest in Regulatory Reform," Alex Potts, *Forbes.com*, April 23, 2010.) State and federally-registered investment advisors are held to a fiduciary standard (no conflict of interest standard), yet stockbrokers are held only to the standard of the suitability of the investment, which is soft on conflicts of interest.

It was a violation of the old common law drawn from Rome and England, codified in the regs, that the SEC resorted to when filing charges against Goldman Sachs a few years before this printing. ". . . The[credit default swap] product was new and complex but the deception[fraud] and conflicts [conflicts of interest law] are old and simple," said Robert Khuzami, Director of the Division of Enforcement of the SEC. The regulation was obviously redundant. The common law was already in place.It ended with the firm owing one of the biggest fines in the history of the Security and Exchange Commission. That wrong was not co-opetition at work: it was über competition at work.

Clearly, regulation stands on the forced-cooperative side of the equation, while non-regulation is on the competitive side. Just as clearly, there is a proper point of synthesis for these factors. Too much regulation invariably chokes off an economy, while too little regulation allows raiders, rip-off artists and other white-collar criminals a free hand. Neither exaggeration leads to *the synthesis.*

It follows, therefore, that business achievement, attained under reasonable ethical standards and proper play is a good and natural thing. It is natural because business practices themselves have evolved in response to changing social principles throughout the history of mankind. After all, if ethics in business were unnatural, standard practices and entire economic systems would never have developed as they have and the perpetual competition for resources through war, raiding and crime would be the only way for societies to exist. Clearly, true capitalism is the supreme example of co-opetition at work.

THE BEST FORM OF DEMOCRACY

Absolute power corrupts absolutely. That syndrome bubbles out in the wonderful movie *Ruby Sparks,* staring Zoe Kazan, who plays the girlfriend, and Paul Dano, who plays the young author/boyfriend.

The girl, a figment of his writing imagination, becomes real. He finds her in his bachelor kitchen one morning cooking his breakfast. In one scene, the author/boyfriend discovers that he can control the personality of his girlfriend by a mere stroke of the pen. He can change her into a French-speaking girl instantly. He dearly loves his girl, yet finds himself gleefully tormenting her. He abuses his absolute power. Why? What makes this seemingly nice man turn sadistic for no apparent reason? What triggered this innate proclivity for despotism?

In my novel, *The Tortoise Shell Game,* and in this book, I show that the founders of the USA were so concerned about absolute power corrupting absolutely that they separated the powers of government into the three branches: administrative, legislative and judicial. They also put in place all sorts of checks and balances: e.g., state's rights versus the federal government; the House of Representatives versus the Senate, among many others. They purposely designed tugs of war in all directions so that no one individual or group could gain absolute power. So perhaps we should rethink the lament, "Why can't we all get along?"

Under co-opetition, too much cooperation can be bad; it can slide toward *forced* cooperation and eventually even dictatorship. We've learned that we need both competition and cooperation in any formula for good government or good living. It takes a synthesis of those behaviors to drive a good political system, or any system. The genius of the U.S Founders is vividly illustrated by this concept of the separation of powers, and of checks and balances. They put into place the necessary elements of *the synthesis.*

In October of 2013, Senator Cruz, occasionally assisted by other Republican Senators, held the floor for 21 hours, 19 minutes, an effort that would earn third place on the list of the longest filibusters in Senate history—if it was a filibuster at all. (Robert Longley, 9-27-13. Did Senator Cruz 'Filibuster' or Not?, About.com, U.S. Government Info.) He was trying to defund the Affordable Healthcare Act, and there was controversy about shutting down the government.

What no one seemed to talk about at the time, however, is that when the country was established, the Founders gave the U.S. Congress and, more particularly, the House of Representatives, a trump card. The Founders handed the purse-strings of the U.S. Treasury only to Congress —Article I, Section 9, Clause 7 (the Appropriations Clause) and Article I, Section 8, Clause 1 (the Taxing and Spending Clause). They didn't give that power to the President.

By bestowing this power over the expenditures of the government's money, the Founding Fathers intended for Congress to act as watchdog over the money. The founders gave Congress, in effect, the power to shut down the government if they didn't like the way the money was being spent. This was their clear intent. An idle act it was not.

Congress not only had the right, but perhaps, the moral duty, to protect those funds. To have acted in good faith, the Executive Branch may have reciprocally had the moral duty to negotiate even over the Affordable Health Care Act to avoid a government shutdown. But it was adamant: it would talk, but not to negotiate any changes.

So the mainstream press, in their commentary, either ignorant of, ignoring, or oblivious to the fact that the Founding Fathers had intentionally given the purse-strings' trump card only to the Congress, fully assessed the blame to the Republicans for the temporary government shutdown. And the conservatives and their pundits apparently did not know their constitutional history well enough to adequately point out the perhaps moral duty on the part of Congress to guard the purse-strings.

In fact, both sides had, at least, the moral duty to in good faith be open to at negotiate whether a change of the act could be accomplished. As it turned out from the later disastrous roll-out of the act, some desired changes may have even benefited the President's launch of the act.

ÜBER-COOPERATION FUELS INEFFICIENCY AND CORRUPTION

The news scandal of the Veteran's Administration's delayed treatment of Vets broke in 2014, too late to make it into the first printing of this book. We discovered that multitudes of patients died while waiting in long queues for admittance to many of the VA hospitals in the U.S. Often, they were killed by the very diseases for which they were awaiting treatment. Administrators sometimes secretly side-tracked Vets for months or more.

The massive cover-ups and corruption that came to light are examples of the horrors that can besiege huge government bureaucracies, especially those trying to manage complex systems—systems that nature would be best suited to simplify. The patients were trapped in a government-forced cooperative VA system. They couldn't go to competing private (or public) hospitals or doctors and obtain reimbursement under the VA rules then in effect. The VA scandal is a microcosm of what could happen under a health care system that smothers the free market and disincentives natural altruism while forcing redistribution and über-complexity.

13

Synthesizing Conservative and Liberal Extremes

The crucial question is: Where does one draw the line between individual liberty and social control? By now you recognize the elements that comprise co-opetition and understand that we should not attempt to dictate precisely where the ultimate synthesis point of a given issue lies.

But we do know certain things. We know that for most issues, the emphasis should be on competition—without forgetting that cooperation is always a necessary ingredient. Positioning the fulcrum should be, therefore, like having a major in competition and a minor in cooperation. But this emphasis is a general rule, which we've shown is not necessarily true in all cases.

THE CLOCK TICKS

Remember that on our clock scale, noon would be the center or balance point between the left and right, and the needle arcs from 9:00 a.m. to 3:00 p.m.

Regarding personal liberty versus group needs, we should start by placing the ultimate synthesis point at noon and then adjust from there as individual cases require. Remember, we are scaling cooperation (collectivism) on the left verses competition (Individualism) on the right. Generally, we should set the initial adjustment asymmetrically a bit to the right because, as said previously, we want to stimulate growth.

As reference points, Communism (world socialism, no borders, no private ownership, total government management, full-on cooperation and forced cooperation, and total order) would be placed at 9:00. Hitler's Nazism and Mussolini's Fascism (both forms of socialism with fully controlled industry in exchange for ensured perpetual profits) are positioned at 9:15, and so-called modern European style socialism at 10:30. Ultraliberals are between 9:10 and 10:00, liberal from 9:45 to 10:45, Democrats from 9:30 to 11:30, and Moderate Democrats from 11:30 to 12:30. Independents can be located in at least two places, 11:00 to 12:00 and 1:30 to 2:30. RINO Republicans would be placed at 11:30 to 12:00. Blue dog Democrats from 11:00 to 12:30. Moderate Republicans would be placed at 12:00 to 1:00, and conservative Republicans from 1:00 to 2:30.

Most Libertarians would be placed between 1:30 and 3:00, with some inconsistent lapses at 11:00 to accommodate, for example, in the areas of drug-legalization, anti-war and advocates of open-border. Given all this, where should we place the ultimate synthesis point on the political systems scale? For America, the ideal position in most situations I would place at from 1:15 to 1:45, for these reasons:

1. You can't have life and growth unless you have competition. So as was said, we should add weight to the competition side. Again, synthesis is not the same as balance; it's a tipping point. It is the sweet spot. It is an asymmetric balance—like is the outrigger canoe.

2. Co-opetition holds that the ideal political system is the republic/democratic form, but one in which the potential for whimsical or tyrannical rule by the majority, by the government, or by a ruler is controlled by a strong charter or constitution. Under this form of democracy, rule by either the majority or the government is tempered by laws protecting the rights of the individual and minorities. Such protections should include, for example, free speech, civil rights, property rights, due process of law, equal application of the law, freedom of religion, and all the protections guaranteed, for example, under the Bill of Rights and the Fourteenth and other Amendments of the U.S. Constitution.

In this way, equal rights and opportunities are provided to all persons, be they dissenters, the socially, politically, physically, or economically-disadvantaged, or the advantaged. Protections would extend to *everyone,* including to those who are financially insecure and those who are secure, i.e. the rich. For example, the Fifth Amendment to the U.S. Constitution provides that government shall not take private property without paying just compensation, and that even then, such taking must be for an appropriate public purpose. Thus, protections extend even to those who may not be favored by the otherwise all-powerful voting majority.

INDIVIDUALITY

It is the protection of individuality that is unique, especially in America. What is individuality? It is competition. It is freedom. It is liberty. Metaphorically, it is a lean toward chaos. Generally speaking, the newly-democratized peoples of Eastern Europe and even Central Europe have not experienced, and don't really understand this "*liberty.*" To this day, it is doubtful that the terms "liberty" and "freedom" evoke the burning passion that it did in the minds of America's founders and in most Americans.

Remember that the ancient Greek philosophers were among the first to be concerned about the tyranny of the majority. They recognized that a form of tyranny happens when the majority takes so much—too much—control of a democratic form of government that they enable themselves to abuse and stomp on the rights of minorities, individuals, or any faction of their choice.

Before the enactment of the Bill of Rights, the U.S. Founding Fathers, including James Madison, the primary writer of the Constitution, tried to control the prospects of majority tyranny by various provisions and concepts. These included checks and balances, the separation of powers between the three branches of government, and the bicameral Senate/Congress form. Also, Senators were originally elected or appointed *not* by popular vote of the states' citizens but by the legislative or executive bodies of each state. Now because of the 17th amendment, Senators are elected by the people of each separate state. Some argue that the amendment weakened the concept of states' rights.

The original constitutional clauses were designed primarily to prevent a potential ruler—be it a king, dictator, the dreaded all-powerful government and its bureaucracies, or simply the whims of the majority of the people—from stomping on the individual. Fictional character Senator Rich Morrison of *The Tortoise Shell Game* explains to the opposing factions at a dramatic mediation of their revolution in Latin America the reasons why the founders here created the separation of powers. They intended that through competition between the powers, *no single faction* could take over the country and become a king or a dictator. The factions necessarily would be compelled to arrive at a synthesis between them.

Over the years since the founding of the U.S. and the passage of the Bill of Rights, which also guaranteed states' rights under the Tenth Amendment, we have seen an erosion of some of those separation- of-powers protections against potential tyranny of the majority. In my view, the unintended consequence has been a creeping path toward subordinating the rights of the individual to the demands of the collective—among other things, a creep toward the welfare state where forced cooperation overburdens competition.

As previously noted, today about 50 percent of the public pays no income taxes—and unless they paid their share of tax "dues" in the past, they ride on the backs of those who do pay. A new immigrant on welfare is a prime example; an illegal immigrant collecting welfare is even worse than that.

Of those who do pay income taxes, due to progressive taxation, the upper 10 percent pay the lion's share by far. With their extra capital, these are the risk takers and investors. Do we really believe the economy can thrive if we tax away their ability to provide investment funds?

This country was founded on the principle of equality under the law. This includes the protection of individuality. In fact, built into the Bill of Rights is the famous provision requiring equal protection under the law for all. Progressive taxation—taking more than a pro-rata proportion from high-earners—was illegal under the Constitution. It was not "equal protection." So, in order to legalize progressive taxing—a form of discrimination against high earners—the country had to amend the Constitution.

In 1913 the government went through an arduous effort to ratify the Sixteenth Amendment. Inconsistently, this happened against our protection of equality under the law.

Once disproportionate income taxation was legalized, taxes for higher earners were raised, in 1932, from 25 percent to 63 percent—the largest tax hike in history. Within the next several years, they were raised even more. Do you think there might have been a correlation between the enablement of disproportionate income taxing by the Sixteenth Amendment, commonly referred to as "progressive taxation," and the later prolongation of the Great Depression of the 1930s when the taxes were jacked so high they were out of sync with rationality?

It's interesting to note that top-bracket income tax rates were fairly low at 25 percent during the ten years of the roaring 1920s (a time when unemployment went as low as 3 percent and annual economic growth was almost 5 percent). But in 1936, the Depression decade of the 1930s—the Roosevelt era—the top bracket tax rates were increased to as high as 79 percent.

All those tax increases pushed the country over the line into too much (forced) cooperation; that is, it pushed too much taxation. Reiterating my previous comments, it was a leading factor as to why the Great Depression languished an additional ten years. (see "Taxes, Depression, and Our Current Troubles," Arthur B. Laffer, *The Wall Street Journal*, September 22, 2009).

What seems to have evolved now through majority vote are

special advantages for social minorities by what has been referred to as "affirmative action." However, there is no concomitant concern for "non-minorities," many of whom are just as financially or socially disadvantaged.

In many jurisdictions, non-minorities have, in both effect and reality, become the minority; they have to fend for themselves without equal protection of the law (see "Court Revives Reverse-Discrimination Suit against Syracuse Involving Fire Department," John O'Brien, *Post-Standard*, August 8, 2010). They have become the victims of reverse discrimination. Cooperation has overburdened competition.

The idea of extending to the advantaged the same protection from the tyranny of the majority as is enjoyed by the disadvantaged seems to have gone out the window. Aren't the advantaged entitled to free speech, freedom of religion, but no longer equal protection of the law? That latter constitutional phrase bars discrimination.

Again, the advantaged do not have the benefit of affirmative action, political correctness, or generally of gaming welfare and other entitlement systems. Of course, the rationale used by Congress is that the advantaged do not *need* protection from the tyranny of the majority. Oh, but they do. If not given such protection, they will lose their ability to compete, and the country could very well wind up a complete welfare or socialist state. Or even worse, the advantaged might then resort to corruption to gain an even playing field and to improve *their* ability to compete. But that would be an illegitimate means of correcting the imbalance, wouldn't it.

What's wrong with that—the full welfare state with corruption to balance the playing field? The answer can be found in history: the goose that laid the golden egg will be destroyed, and the country as it was founded will be extinguished. It will crumble from within, just as happened to Rome and the Republics of Greece—just as happened to the Soviet Union from the beginnings of the Revolution, to 1991.

I believe that as a result of too much emphasis on cooperation (collectivism-über order), the growth of the American government is running out of control. I place the current point of synthesis at about 10:30—whereas it should be between 1:00 and 1:45.

Since co-opetition is a natural condition, synthesis will restore itself by one means or another. In this case, government distortions of political syntheses have resulted in the evolution of more and more illegitimate means of correction. Individuals or organizations with the wherewithal now use money, political pressure, or lobbyists to offset the tyranny of the majority; they—activists and special interests—influence legislators and other members of government to attach last minute undiscussed riders to legislation, often unrelated to the main bill; and sometimes they've attached so-called "earmarks" to appropriation bills, a practice that had grown exponentially until the Republican Congress, to their credit, banned the practice.

Aside from banning earmarks, the general trend is the rise of unintended consequences from the erosion of checks and balances. The government becomes a breeding ground for legalized bribery and increasing levels of corruption.

Rather than easing toward the synthesis point, legislators tend to work in the other direction, piling regulation on top of regulation. I predict that another unintended consequence will eventually result: the further regression and de-evolution of the economic status of the freeloaders and those who game the system. By this I mean that if people use crutches long enough, they won't be able to walk on their own when the crutches are taken away.

Since history shows that no government can perpetually support ever-growing numbers of nonproductive citizens, eventually the handouts will have to end. Unfortunately, by that time, those who have wrung the neck of the goose that lays the golden egg will have also lost their ability to survive by legal means. The result? Increasing crime, decreasing economic power, and greater demands for support from a government less and less able to provide it. Is the chronic economic plight of Greece in 2013 a barometer?

I reflected on this during my travels through the Costa Rican rain forest with a van of tourists. One woman was discussing her concern for the homeless in the big cities of America. She appeared to be in favor of them receiving more of a hammock than a safety net.

We had just left a game station where the rangers had recently had a crisis: the near extinction of a breed of wild monkeys. The rangers then figured out that the monkeys were dying out because tourists and park naturalists had been feeding them. The unintended consequence of this form of over-cooperation? Mother monkeys had forgotten how to teach their young to forage for themselves in the forest; accordingly, without lifelong outside support or retraining, the youngsters began starving to death.

As far as I could tell, my fellow tourist never considered that a possible correlation of the Costa Rican problem to that of *some* of the homeless of America might be made. Please note that I said *some*, not all. I wish to be politically correct here.

The classic book *Atlas Shrugged* by Ayn Rand, published in the early 1950s, foretells much of what has befallen the U.S. since then. Many give the book high marks; other reviewers rabidly denigrate it, some do so strictly on her abilities or inabilities as a writer rather than about her message. In my view, non-literary criticisms stemming from her political views result from bias and are fraught with agenda promotion. The novel is approximately 1,300 pages and, at times, arduous reading. Although written in English, Rand's young-adult Russian life obviously influenced her style—long paragraphs as in the works of Fyodor Dostoyevsky or Chekov, and about as inaccessible.

I read the novel twice (separated by forty years) and saw the recent movie twice. Even the admittedly left-leaning members of my group of friends attending the film with me agreed that the film was quite good. I suspect that the book's critics relied not on a thorough reading of the novel so much as on biased comments from other collectivist-leaning reviewers. As to whether or not *Atlas Shrugged* is true literature, probably not—but I'll defer to the experts on that one.

One point about Ayn Rand's teachings that I referred to earlier and wish to emphasize now is that when speaking about self-interest, she always meant, and usually said, "*rational* self-interest." Most of the time she made the distinction clear with her prose. The word "rational" infers the cooperative part of the equation. The same is true of British Conservative House of Commons member Daniel Hannan, who spoke of "moral liberty," or of conservative Mark Levin, who spoke of "ordered liberty."

I interviewed a young Russian woman who had immigrated to the U.S. and now speaks perfect English. She couldn't say specifically why she considered *Atlas Shrugged* less than worthy. Finally she blurted, "It was simplistic," then admitted she had never read it. I suspect she was speaking under the effects of childhood Communist brainwashing. When she saw the film, she changed her mind.

The story in *Atlas Shrugged* is truly prophetic. It depicts a growing attitude on the part of the well-intentioned government to provide the needy with an outcome equivalent for all—a hammock, you might say, rather than a safety net. Soon the minority becomes the majority and became utterly dependent on the government. The government then believed that it must take over the operation and management of industry. The industrialists and capitalists dropped out and faded away, and soon the whole system collapsed. Factories burn in the ensuing riots. Everyone starves.

At the end, the people who had figured out what was happening—the industrious ones, the innovative ones—reestablish their own secret enclave under the leadership of John Galt and start over.

I see Rand as intending to portray John Galt as a metaphor, or symbol, for a person who finally "gets it." For example: a conservative Ronald Reagan had been a left-leaning Hollywood union boss. Conservative author David Horowitz had been a radical left-wing activist during Vietnam war era. Among many others, they both proclaimed that they *did* finally "get it" and became conservative. Each could have been the modern day John Galt. They lived and saw the best and the worst of both philosophies— left and right—and became passionate opponents of collectivism-socialism. I find that to be extremely compelling evidence of where lies the truth. The wisdom gained from experience often filters truth from raw passion. Passion with no wisdom could lead to fire on the floor.

Leo, a coffee-shop conversationalist I know, served in the Russian army as a tank commander. With his Soviet counterparts, he drove his tank through the flaming streets of Budapest, Hungary during the Russian invasion of 1956. You should hear him lament about Marxism and his dread that the U.S. may be softening to the collectivist idea. His desire for freedom brought him to America—a country he regarded as the last bastion of liberty, but which now he feels is fading from that heralded position.

The Capitalist Manifesto by Andrew Bernstein is another good book to read. He writes of the history of free enterprise and capitalism. I tried to find an explanation in the text for the existence of altruism or something akin to the cooperative aspects of coopetition, but did not find anything that satisfied me at the time. But now I believe the answer is very simple and clear. I am reminded that "capitalism" has within it—as does "free enterprise"—a built-in cooperative behavior trait that enables capitalism to work: the intuition of ethics and morality.

Again, this is more or less Adam Smith's Invisible Hand: i.e. "a major in competition and a minor in cooperation"—maintaining the co-opetition synthesis in an asymmetric balance, primarily as governed by nature.

In *Guns, Germs and Steel,* and in *Collapse: How Societies Choose to Fail or Succeed,* Jared M. Diamond, PhD., wrote about prehistoric cultures and what caused their advancement, differences, and collapses. He spoke of bands growing to tribes, into chiefdoms and then to states. Bands were mostly egalitarian; family groups of 20 or so people or less, no long-term real leader, and decisions usually made by the community. Tribes were characterized by stronger leadership via the "Big-Man" power shifts; yet, they still shared food, hunting grounds, and resources.

At the other extreme were the states, mostly kleptocracies (run by thieves), generally of more than 200,000 people, which had definite leaders, often with inherited power such as royalty/ emperors; enforced with the aid of a belief in organized religion; often slavery was a part of the system. Kleptocracy connotes the idea of tribute paid by the subjects to the leader, i.e. a form of theft by him, in Diamond's view.

How does co-opetition apply? You would think that egalitarian means cooperative, whereas kleptocracy would mean an emphasis in competition. But no, both systems entail forms of cooperation. Kleptocracy is forced-cooperation. This is so because you would find co-opetition in both types of society. But the fulcrum point for leadership would shift considerably for each type. Was the sweet spot for survival achieved? It must have been or humankind would have become extinct.

When the society grows to the size of a state, there is evidence of great food production, much tool-making and trade, all forms of industry and technology—that is, as I interpret it, primitive forms of capitalism. Yet, Diamond refers to leadership of a state as a kleptocracy, a negative term connoting thievery and forced-co-operation. Is he separating the political-leadership aspects of the prehistoric state from the economic-capitalist aspects? And is he talking only of prehistoric states or is he analogizing to the modern state or any state? I must conclude that Diamond assumes—or equates—the attitudes of those who ran or run states, i.e. countries, ipso facto to have been, or are, of thieves.

Yes, that was, and is often the case, but not always. Not when you have a country that was founded on what I term the coopetition principles, as was the United States. The Founders, however, rightly knew those principles as the Age of Reason philosophies. In the U.S, true thieves as leaders would have been jailed many times over. Not much of that occurred. In actuality very few have been. Diamond is implicitly saying that the capitalism aspect when grown to the size of a state is necessarily, or inherently, evil—i.e. that capitalists are thieves.

After all, he termed state systems kleptocracy. It seems his sphere of reference does not compel him to apply Adam Smith's Invisible Hand to the workings of capitalism, prehistoric or otherwise, nor of Ayn Rand's *rational* self-interest, Hannon's *ordered* liberty, Levin's *moral* liberty, nor Asaro's *coopetition*. Rather than concluding that states are kleptocracies, the question to ask is which society has the most or the least freedom for its members?

As I read Diamond, the most freedom would be characteristic of the bands, which had no real dictator. On the other hand, the state would most likely be controlled by royalty, an emperor, or dictator. That system would be characterized with the ultimate forced–cooperative condition. The key is, again, which society gives the most liberty to the individual?

In its extreme form, which is closest to anarchy with no leadership, as opposed to which is closest to dictatorship-police state with one or few supreme leaders? Or in other words, which type of political-economic system accomplishes coopetition? The answer: republican democracy is a method of supplying co-opetition. It is a system that is intuitively designed to give liberty (competition) to the individual while (cooperatively) unifying the group. It is an equation of the *competition of liberty* with the *cooperation of societal order*. It then becomes a matter of finding the sweet spot in synthesizing liberty with control, i.e. between the freedom of individuality and the interests of the group as a whole.

We can help decipher what was going on in the development and sustenance of Diamond's prehistoric societies by analogizing them to today's typical business firm of working partners or members. Whether it is a band, tribe, chiefdom, or a state, the natural tendency is for the firm to pay or distribute to the member-partners their fair share of what they earn for the firm. If they contribute little value, they have not earned their keep. In prehistoric times, in such a case, a non-producing member would probably have been ostracized or driven to homelessness. It is an implied contract between the firm and the member.

So we extrapolate that in modern times, when we speak of a safety-net social system for those who cannot contribute anything of value to themselves or to the group, we are actually talking about pure altruism, based solely on an innate empathy or charity, stemming from the cooperative extreme of nature's equation. No nation can support more than a limited number of people who contribute nothing of value to their society.

In those prehistoric societies of bands and tribes, Diamond implies that the motivation was either egalitarian, or it was redistribution. He does not suggest that there is a third system: pure capitalism. There a primary motive is profit but according to Adam Smith, profit achieved ethically. If not so achieved, business (trade) would grind to a halt. Such is profit achieved by way of co-opetition. Such would not mean redistribution (taking from the producers and giving to the non-producers) because the members of such a prehistoric society would have necessarily truly earned their share of the capitalist, socio-economic pie.

Redistribution, on the other hand, connotes that the member gets a piece of the socio-economic pie whether he earns it or not. Such has never worked as an economic system and never will work. I very much doubt that it worked in prehistoric times either.

Why did many societies eventually collapse? Diamond talks of two reasons. They had conflicts of interest and could not adapt. His key examples were the Vikings who settled Greenland for 400 years before finally fading away, and the Easter Islanders of the south eastern Pacific who fell into drastic decline. How do we apply the concept of co-opetition to societal collapse?

The conflict of interest reason stemmed from allowing short term needs and greeds to outweigh long term considerations, one being conservation. The Easter Islanders cut down all their palm tree forests, which were necessary for making their ocean-going canoes. They eventually found themselves with no boats from which to bring in fish. They didn't conserve and allow replenishment of the palm forest. The short term desire was selfish and individualistic and with too much competition.

On the other hand, long term or conservation considerations would mean cooperation for the sake of the future, for the descendants, for posterity. The hands of the clock face were way over to 3:00. They did not find the sweet spot between the two.

There is an important caveat to the Easter Island story, though. Recent documentaries have argued that the Easter Islanders did not commit so-called "eco-suicide." The main suspected culprit: disease. A Dutch sailing ship had visited the Easter Islands on Easter Sunday, 1722, that occurring perhaps 48 years prior to the Spanish landing there and Captain Cooks arrival about four years after the Spanish. The Dutch had found the natives living in ordinary abundance, of perhaps 10,000 in population, surrounded with mostly cultivated vegetation. It is theorized that this seemingly benign state lasted only as long as it took for disease from the Dutch ship to become unleashed and decimate the native population. For, when the Spanish and Cook later arrived, they came upon a vastly smaller population than had existed at the time of the Dutch ship. And, by then, there was very little cultivation.

Apparently, competing microbes from the Dutch ship outbalanced the benign, non-competitive microbes of the natives. The bubble of existence of the natives did not offer sufficient competition from the foreign microbes. The section in this book on why utopia may not be a good thing is further demonstrative of this point of the hazards of living in a bubble.

Regarding the 400 year old Viking colony in Greenland: as the climate changed and got colder during the Little Ice Age, the colonists didn't adapt as did the Inuit who lived nearby. The Vikings clung to their Christian traditions and did not stay loose enough to adopt the Inuit's methods. Such is an example of too much cooperation on the part of the colonists. Too much group-think, based on tradition—not enough competition and change to adapt to the demands of survival. They didn't effectuate an attitude of . . . "survive now," rather than hoping that tradition-God-custom would save them. In this respect they had the hands of their clock face way over to 9:00—to much cooperation.

At the end of Guns, Germs and Steel, Diamond compares China with Euro-American Renaissance and industrial revolution era. China was for centuries ruled by huge dynasties, whereas Europe consisted of an array of city states, especially in the Italian peninsula. More competition between the multitudes of societies, including from burgeoning capitalism, he attributes as the reason why Europe (and America) surpassed China in technology at that stage. I see this as more evidence of coopetition at work. In China there was more influence of forced-cooperation through the big dynasties, whereas in Europe and America there was more competition, which engendered attitudes of freedom to invent.

Prior to the 15th century and the beginning of the renaissance China had technologically surged ahead of Europe, but after that juncture in time it was Europe's turn to advance past China. In other words, it was the super-unification (forced cooperation) of the Chinese people under huge dynasties that restrained innovation in China, while at the same time it was the fragmentation of Europe into small competing city-states and factions that spurred innovative competition in Europe, enabling it to forge ahead of China technologically.

At that point Europe was closer to the sweet spot between competing and cooperating—between the mass unification of

China's dynasties, versus the relative disunity of the European peoples. In short, in Europe, competition served to develop more freedom and innovation than existed at that time in China. By further analogy I remind the reader that in 1776 Adam Smith, in his Wealth of Nations treatise, attributed the rise of capitalism in North America to the passion of the colonists for greater freedom—including greater freedom for trade and innovation. That is why, as he said, the American economy was well on its way to surpassing the economies of all other nations.

THE CONSERVATIVE EXTREME

For the conservative extreme, the clock-face scale is currently set too far to the right—almost, in fact, at 2:45. The ultraconservative idea of totally unrestrained economic competition and unchecked free enterprise without meaningful social cooperation, does not accomplish the synthesis required by nature. A safety-net of programs including local public education, local basic welfare, Social Security; senior, catastrophic, and indigent medical care; local health and safety protection, local crime control, necessary public works, parks, a modicum of apolitical public art, music, drama, and literature is also necessary. Anti-monopoly laws should also be retained and enforced.

Because the ultimate synthesis-scale sweet spot is generally found at around 1:15, there is room here for wise regulation. I define "wise regulation" as regulation that does not allow freeloaders to abuse the system, keeps a watchful eye on burgeoning bureaucracies, and does regulation without choking the economy. For we know that no matter how good the intensions, ill-conceived plans lead down the road to hell.

Bureaucrats have a tendency to embrace and form symbiotic relationships with freeloaders or with inefficient, obsolete programs. Their motivation is to protect their political jobs, expand their agencies, and personal power, thereby growing their fiefdoms. With the help of public employees' unions, tainted with conflict of interest, the bureaucrats boost their salaries, benefits, and pensions. This issue is more fully detailed in subsequent chapters.

Last and most important, there must be regulations to prevent the "financing" of government programs by the redistribution of funds. Redistribution is not finance; it is a form of raiding— something practiced by uncivilized tribes in prehistoric times. We must utilize *true* finance, such as from bonds, debentures, annuities, trust investments, and U.S. Treasuries, and many other financial instruments.

Of course, bureaucrats build their fiefdoms at the expense of the innocent silent majority of the people and to the detriment of their country. The natural tendency for bureaucrats, either consciously or non-consciously, is to expand by exponential proportions the number of people dependent on government programs and hand-outs. This leads to the growth of inefficient, unneeded, or obsolete programs. Why should it be acceptable to pay a greater number of government workers to do the job that one private sector worker can do?

The Affordable Health Care Act rollout problems at the end of 2013 is illustrative of what can happen with government bureaucrats in charge. In the private sector, the person in charge can be fired for similar incompetence. "Have you tried to get on the Obamacare website?" said Jay Leno. "Oh, it's slow! It's so slow that by the time you sign up for Obamacare you'll be eligible for Medicare."

SYNTHESIS POINT FOR ECONOMIC SYSTEMS

Where should we place the synthesis fulcrum in order to achieve the most desirable economic system? Where is the sweet spot? Certainly we should place it well to the right of noon. Without competitors and risk-takers the economy would grind to a halt, likely resulting in economic depression and upheaval.

The movers and shakers, the capitalists and even the moneyed power-elite are the people who provide the majority of productive jobs. Government must not overregulate and stifle them. To do so would cause the story of *Atlas Shrugged* to come *completely* true instead of just largely true, as it already has.

Let's return to the metaphor of the outrigger canoe. Sleek and asymmetrically balanced, the main hull of the canoe houses individuality, free enterprise, liberty—all on the competition side—in the main hull of the vessel. On the other hand, the outrigger—the much smaller pontoon—contains regulation, government bureaucracy, and forced or involuntary cooperation. The fulcrum—the sweet spot—is located on the spars close to the main hull.

The spars hold the outrigger pontoon at a safe distance and is there only to keep the canoe from capsizing in a gale. As a whole, the outrigger canoe symbolizes economic co-opetition with the emphasis weighted on the competition side.

The recent works of two political science/philosophical writers I've discussed earlier in this book depict the ideal political systems very well. See their wonderful books: *Tyranny and Liberty*, by Mark Levin, and *The New Road to Serfdom*, by Daniel Hannon.

To reiterate, Levin talks of "ordered liberty." As I've said, "order" is another way of referring to "cooperation," and "liberty" is another way of saying "competition." Hannon refers to John Winthrop's 1643 description of the desired American political system as "moral liberty." In my view, "moral" implies cooperation, whereas "liberty" is a form of competition. Regardless, both terms describe co-opetition with an emphasis on competition.

WHO ARE THE GREEDY ONES?

Carrying the outrigger analogy a little further, let's say the wind dies, and we must all paddle. When we work cooperatively we make great speed. Let's say some of us are infirm and cannot paddle. We move those people to the back of the boat. Let's say some other paddlers do not work as hard and long as others. Soon it dawns on the sweating leaders that some of those in the boat are getting a free ride off the labors of others. The lazy or crafty individuals are gaming the system.

The boat slows and eventually stops. Those who are greedy— *truly* greedy—are those who, although capable of working, choose to ride on the backs of the productive ones. Unchallenged, they will become like the native monkeys in the Costa Rican wild park who forgot how to forage for themselves; they become dependent on being fed by the tourists—i.e. by the working taxpayers.

DEMOCRACY, THE TYRANNY OF THE MAJORITY, AND THE PHILOSOPHER KING

Expanding on subjects reviewed earlier in this work, the ancient philosophers, including Socrates and Plato, were concerned about controlling the tyranny of the majority. They feared that the majority could at times develop a herd or mob mentality and take advantage of the minority (e.g., the Salem Witch Trials, Old West lynch mobs, massive mob action during the French Revolution, the Los Angeles riots, etc.)

The concept of the tyranny of the majority was not lost on James Madison, Thomas Jefferson, and the other Founders of the United States of America. One of the primary reasons for the enactment of the Bill of Rights (later expanded by the Fourteenth Amendment, among others) and for the checks and balances that are built into the U.S. Constitution, was to provide safeguards against all forms of abuse that may be committed by the majority. Another equally important reason for those safeguards is to protect the people from abuse by the government and its leaders.

This is why in any political system, the rules advocated by the majority are not necessarily best. The majority view may tailor law only to benefit the majority, or the masses. It can become out-of-balance through massive cooperation, forced cooperation, or the adoption of mob or herd mentality; the result is the restriction of individual freedoms. Such restrictions are signposts of too much cooperation, or of forced cooperation out-tipping competition.

Remember: at one stage the majority of citizens in Germany willingly followed Hitler and his socialist/ fascist views. Excessive cooperation (or forced-cooperation) on the one hand, and runaway competition on the other, will each generally result in disproportionate swings to the far right or to the far left. Swings to the left can produce a police state; swings to the right can be produce anarchy.

WHY PAST DEMOCRACIES FAILED

Founding father James Madison believed he had discovered why most previous democracies had ended in decline: when the majority figures out it can loosen the purse-strings of government, it spends all the money. This is why the great political philosopher Alexis De Tocqueville once said, "The American Republic will endure until the day Congress discovers that it can bribe the public with the public's money." We'll call it "a government playing Santa Claus to stay in power."

This is the main reason the Greek philosophers had some doubts about garden variety democracy, and preferred the Philosophers King-controlled government. It comes down to avoiding the risk that the majority will spend all the money. So you come up with a Republic-type democracy with a strong charter to ensure a control against spending all the money in the treasury and to ensure civil rights to all, including the minority. You accomplish this by adding some competition, some minority balance, against the unfettered whims of the majority.

A common theme of waning democracies has been weak financial status, that is, they are going broke. Sometimes they spend too much on wars or sometimes too much on the social welare of the majority or all of the above. The Romans financed wars and financed welfare to their populous including through entertainment by handing out wheat and financing gladiator and circus shows in the coliseums.

Julius Caesar crossed the Rubicon because, among other reasons, he wanted more order among the populace and the provinces and he wanted to control the treasury. Thus he proclaimed himself dictator, and eventually abandoned the concept of the Republic.

This "run on the treasury" proclivity by the majority is a big deal when trying to operate a democracy. The democracy will go bankrupt if the purse strings are not wisely administered. Greece never learned. Look at her financial status as of 2015. The people became addicted to the government being their Santa Claus. Generally, see "The Failure of Democracy and the Rise of the Welfare State," by Camille Pecastaing—May 3, 2013, *Real Clear Politics*

In republics and democracies previous to the U.S., all of which ended in failure, financial issues usually played an important role in their demise. Often the politicians and the majority of citizens thoughtlessly bankrupted their own government. In those failed systems, sufficient checks and balances against the whims of the majority had not been established or, if established, were not enforced by the people, the courts or, even more importantly, by an independent, knowledgably competent and diligent press.

Recall the Alexis De Tocqueville quote: "The American Republic will endure until the day Congress discovers that it can bribe the public with the public's money." In ancient Rome they had a mechanism to convert to a dictatorship for brief periods in order to solve crisies and to get something done. Generally, financial stress of the government and its failure to provide public services was often the causation of the failure of the democracy. (Generally see Dictatorships for Democracy: Takeovers of Financially Failed Cities, Clayton P. Gillette.)

As previously stated, part of the checks and balances system in the U.S. requires that control of the nation's purse-strings be given only to the House of Representatives, not the Senate (except indirectly to a lesser extent) nor to the President.

Not only does the House have the right to withhold money from problematic spending programs, the Founders intended for the House to have the *ethical duty* to guard against waste, and that is implicit in their mandate to be the controller of the purse-strings.

By the same token, when the House cinches the purse tight, the President and Senate have the good-faith obligation to at least engage in negotiation with the House to attempt to convince it—or to work a compromise with it—to allow for the particular funding in question.

ILLEGAL IMMIGRATION, DIFFERING
CULTURES, AND ETHNICITIES

Here the clock scale is at 10:00 and we should change our national policies to place the hand back to 2:00. With illegal immigration streaming in from all the countries of the Middle East, Europe, Mexico, Central America, China, South Africa, Canada, Israel, and many other regions, the American melting pot has lately been brimming over with no time to melt, assimilate or integrate.

The 2015 San Francisco murder of beautiful young Kate Steinle by an illegal alien who'd been convicted of multiple felonies and had been deported 5 times brought national attention to the practice of providing sanctuary to illegals by certain cities in the U.S. See generally the article: *Trump is Right: Illegal Alien Crime is Staggering in Scope and Savagery* by the team at Family Security Matters, July 10, 2015 The article states that *Non-Americans commit over five times more serious crimes per capita than Americans.* The specious attempt to justify the Sanctuary Cities policy argues that witnesses would be more apt to report crimes if they needn't fear deportation for coming forward. The simple answer for that is to give the witness immunity from prosecution, including for violation of immigration laws, for coming forward. And the law to do that is already on the books. Immunity from prosecution is a common practice. Under the law, the prosecuting authority is able to give a U-Visa to any such undocumented person or potential witness. An illustration may be found in the *Tortoise Shell Game* novel: El Gato is given immunity when he comes back to the U.S. to testify on behalf of Anthony Darren. Resorting to a "sanctuary city" policy is pure sophistry from the "no borders" crowd. The authority is able to tailor protection for the undocumented witness. There is no need for a so-called sanctuary city policy.

I am referring only to *illegal* immigration. The parameters of legal immigration were established on criteria relating to measured growth and the absorption rate preferred by the American people—the melting pot. Over the past forty years, however, assimilation into our culture has, in many cases, not had time to fully mature. The fault lies with three main culprits: big business seeking cheap labor, unions seeking new members, and Democrats seeking voters. This is where some Republicans, most Democrats, and a naive press gang together and, for the sake of greed and naivety, ruin the country, its economy, and its culture.

Regarding culture, for example, Adam Smith's philosophy concerning mutual benefit to both sides of the economic equation is more understood in the U.S. than in some other countries. Capitalism or free-enterprise as Adam Smith envisioned will not work without a culture of ethics as part of the equation. For some foreign groups, there is more tolerance in their native lands for the idea of bribery than here in the U.S. Many cultures believe that corruption is just another way of doing business. As a result, many traditional Americans now fear that such transplanted mores are eroding the ethics of traditional American business and culture.

In relation to erosion of ethics in politics of late, "a record 46 percent of Americans think Congress is 'corrupt. The other 54 percent think Congress is '*extremely* corrupt,'" says Jay Leno.

I learned from one-on-one discussions with a Ukrainian woman, and from personal experience in Mexico City, among other countries and encounters, that something akin to anarchy is the brand of freedom that some of those people find themselves relegated. In some areas of Latin America, the word "*Mordida*" is famous. It means, *the bite, the bribe.*

Where Mafia-type corruption infects government. People

must rely on their own resources or must pay a quiet "fee" to the authorities to get redress or to get "equal protection of the law." We've heard stories of, not only the so-called Mexican Mafia, but also the Russian, the Hungarian and other Eastern European "mafias"

On a trip to Mexico City in my late teens, I saw steel blocks rise out of the street, right in the main intersection of the city, to stop traffic at a red light. The light alone was not enough.

I recall the trip a few buddies and I made to Cabo San Lucas, Mexico for deep sea fishing some years ago. As we were returning, a strike of airlines in the U.S. caught us at the La Paz airport. No flights back could be found. The owner of a private two engine Navaho Piper offered us a ride. His plane sat perhaps six or seven persons. But he was waiting for a new magnito part for his plane to show up at the postal warehouse. He had to repair a problem before we could take off. For three days he kept going to the warehouse, checking, then tellimg us that they couldn't find the part; they told him that perhaps it hadn't arrived yet.

One of our group asked him whether he had offered the desk clerk a tip. He seemed surprised at the suggestion. He immediately went back down to the warehouse and came back with the magnito part. When he offered a tip of perhaps forty dollars, they found the part immediately.

I found in Iquitos, Peru near the headwaters of the Amazon, there was a frontier ambiance, almost no cars—only bicycle-wheeled rickshaws regularly pulled or motor-scootered on the wrong side, or any side, of the street. Many years ago in Mazara del Vallo, Italy, on the island of Sicily, a huge traffic jam with yells and honking horns persisted at the main cross section in the middle of the city. They had turned off the light signal because no one stopped on red.

So, we see more individual competition to get justice or to escape regulation, but we see, perhaps necessarily, more compulsory cooperation from forceful governments, to control crime—to control this semblance of anarchy.

In the short run in the U.S., what is the answer to this seeming problem of erosion of ethics, which some believe correlates in part to a clash of cultures due to illegal immigration? First, drastically slow, if not stop, illegal immigration—from wherever it emanates. Turn off the attraction lanterns and prosecute those who hire illegals. Such employers undermine American wages; they are illegitimate. They are of the same morality as athletes who take drugs to gain advantage over competitors.

The difference in the immigration policies between Norway and Sweden are illustrative. As a result of the recent Iraq and Afghanistan wars, many refugees were allowed sanctuary in liberal Sweden. Not so much in Norway. In Sweden, the unintended consequence of the surge in immigration is the almost overwhelming burden now shouldered by the formerly ample resources of the government there. Native Swedes, who generally regard accepting government social help as shameful unless absolutely necessary, are scrambling to correct the problem. Concern there is rising. Is this an example of cooperation by the government being too great, competition by the Swedes themselves too weak, and co-opetition failing? ("Sweden's immigration system under strain from surge in Syrian refugees." *Associated Press*, January 30, 2013.)

At the neighborhood coffee shop recently, the discussion de jour included the various interruptions of construction of the United States-Mexico border fence. It is in varied stages of completion across portions of the southern border. One companion stated that the fence "prevented Mexican illegal aliens from leaving the U.S. to return to their homeland." We all knew that argument was preposterous. For a hundred years, no guards on the Mexican side ever, to my knowledge, stood in the way or even checked travelers in that direction, especially at the Tijuana entry station.

But then we quickly realized that he meant that if the fence were completed and put into use, illegal aliens who were considering going home for a short stay would simply not take the chance of leaving the U.S. because the fence might prevent their return back to America. Therefore the fence would do no good.

This is the kind of failure of logic that misunderstands synthesis. If illegal immigrants leave the U.S. with the intention of returning and later do so, they never really left at all! They have simply resumed their status as illegal aliens in the U.S.

My coffee companion argued that he was referring to illegals departing America who might change their minds about returning once they'd left; that didn't make sense either. Those who take the chance of leaving and returning in the face of a border fence cancel those who would have left and returned because there was no boarder fence. Moreover, those who return because there is no fence are more likely to bring relatives with them.

The purpose of the fence is to prevent new illegals from entering the U.S., not to prevent existing illegals from leaving. The Mexicans certainly don't prevent their citizens from re-entering their country. Building the fence and enforcing the nation's borders is evidence of competition. The failure of federal authorities to fully enforce border security is evidence of excessive, über-cooperation. This is where big business hungering for cheap labor, unions hungering for new members, and left-leaning politicians and bureaucrats hungering for new voters and bigger fiefdoms gang up on the on majority of the public.

My coffee conversationalist retorted that the Great Wall of China proved to be ineffective. Actually this is substantially untrue, although certainly there were breaches at times. For great periods the wall was very effective. For many years, it held back Mongol invasions, and later, the Ming Dynasty effectively used the Wall again. When the Manchus breached it in the 1600s, it was because they had bribed the sentries to let them in.

Similarly, the completion and maintenance of Hadrian's Wall in northern England by the Romans between the years 55 and 450 A.D. coincided with one of Britain's longest periods of relative peace, upwards of 400 years.

Many of the Hispanics who live *legally* in the U.S. are opposed to *illegal* aliens crashing in. They undercut jobs, as gardener and family man David Gomez asserts. He has been out of work for months. Similarly, Bob, a licensed contractor with a family in San Diego, told me he has been out of construction jobs for a year. The other day an acquaintance finally offered to let him bid on a house-painting job. He bid three thousand dollars, including paint, which effectively amounted to the return of his costs plus minimum wage. The acquaintance informed him that he'd been outbid by illegal aliens who ended up doing a slightly less professional job, but for only nine hundred dollars.

The benefits we accord our elderly, poor, sick, and handicapped, which include those reasonably incapable of surviving on their own, are not, and cannot be, available to the entire 7 billion people of the planet. If we tried to support the entire world, we would quickly sink beneath the human tsunami. It is ironic that those of us more concerned with our exponential population growth are the first to support politicians who do nothing to secure the border. Lax or insincere border security is an invitation for crashers to enter the country, increasing our nation's population, generally with unskilled workers.

Unsecured borders provide a safety-valve to the people of those areas of the globe not able or not willing to resist over-population. We must limit and control our borders. We must keep our U.S. raft afloat for our nation-selves and for those who have a right to be here. (We can give some help to the rest, but must not allow them to illegally land on our shores and inundate our nation-raft.) The look-the–other–way politicians receive special-interest financial campaign support from certain lobbies.

As said before, at least four powerful self-interest groups combine to gang up on our nation; they force illegal immigration upon us. They are: certain big businesses who want cheap labor, certain unions who want new members, certain minorities who want more of their culture to become a bigger future voting bloc, and in general, the Democratic Party because it will garner the vast majority of the future vote of the illegal immigrants when they get the right to vote.

For the most part, illegal immigrants have not known our culture and system of liberty that exists here. They are used to subjugation by government, by the state. Big government is what they are used to. If we do a better job of controlling our borders, the supply of cheap labor will lessen and wages of the unskilled here will go to higher without the necessity of distorting the free market by raising the minimum wage.

The Children

As to how to humanely deal with the children of illegal immigrants, the innocent victims of such anarchy, I defer to those wiser than I. However, applying the equation of co-opetition should be a good start.

THOUGHTS ON U.S. ROLE IN WORLD ECONOMY

Since the end of World War I, the U.S. economy, in general, has been to the earth what the giant, roiling red spot wind storm is to planet Jupiter. It stimulates the economies of the entire world. However because of our subsequent government policies of über-cooperation, that great churning economic spot has at times fallen out of balance, triggering more than one worldwide crisis.

We've discussed some of the best-known examples: the artificially prolonged Great Depression of the 1930s, which was essentially the unintended consequence of government interference with the free market. Among other factors, for example, if wages had been allowed to edge downward in step with the drop of prices, comparably more workers would have been hired. Instead, wages were kept artificially high by the Civil Service and labor-monopolist unions. Thus, unemployment rose higher than the free market would have allowed. (see "Taxes, Depression, and Our Current Troubles," Arthur B. Laffer).

In the same way, as we said earlier, the Great World Recession that began in late 2008 was triggered mainly by the collapse of the sub-prime mortgage bubble. That bubble resulted from yet another misguided governmental social-engineering policy where it promoted home ownership for low-income buyers who simply could not afford the homes they chose. Of course this disaster later became exacerbated by fraud on Wall Street—a fraud from which the government for years looked the other way (see *Reckles$ Endangerment*, Gretchen Morgenson and Joshua Rosner, 2011).

Those foreigners—or even naive Americans—who wish to see the economic weakening of the U.S. to help level the world's economic playing field should carefully review their reasoning; they might unknowingly be seeking the demise of the very engine—the giant red spot—that still powers the greatest portion of the world's economy.

As the driving force of the world economy, the U.S. provided a bulwark against the European-style socialistic economies that were popular following World War II. Most of these economies—for example, those of Greece and England—stubbornly and anachronistically persisted on their course. Those economies would have fully collapsed long ago had the U.S. not been economically dominant enough to help pull the wagon for all the rest and keep them from languishing into a continuum of grey socialism ("grey socialism" is prophecy in *Atlas Shrugged*).

In the U.K., a reprieve occurred during Margaret Thatcher's term, and now other economies are beginning to discover, and some have already learned, the hard lessons. Ironically, here in the U.S., the "Statists" (those espousing super-big government) and Utopians seem bent, unintentionally or by design, on dragging our country into the same drain that sucked down Greece.

Socialism is a dated, obsolete drain from which most of the emerging economies of the world are trying to escape. But the U.S. presently seems blind to the "Don't go there" signposts, even as she meets wised-up travelers on the way back.

The promising bottom line, however, is that there are countries that choose to carry forward with "co-opetitionist" economies, adding to the free-enterprise phalanx still spearheaded—albeit with blunted head—by the U.S. This will foster a new synergy, raising all ships, thereby shifting momentum closer to a good, pragmatic economy.

An über-cooperative "utopia" that traditional Leftists have fumbled to find and never will is not what we want or need.

Those governments will go extinct from the attempt by gradually self-destructing. Such failure results because of a misguided obsession with anachronistic, illogical, über-cooperative Marxism and socialism—man-made systems that do not allow Mother Nature to work her magic.

Socialism, I re-emphasize, is based on *redistribution* of wealth ("From each according . . ."); capitalism is based on *building* wealth. One is a Ponzi scheme with no fund to build or end up with; the other invests money to earn exponentially more money. Trying to meld them together is proverbially like trying to mix water and oil. Sooner or later, redistribution fails every time.

WHAT 'S THE PROBLEM WITH GOVERNMENT EMPLOYEE UNIONS?

On this subject, the scale is at a problematic 10:00. The point of synthesis should be moved all the way back to 1:45. Ask Governor Scott Walker of Wisconsin, a generally liberal state, about his experience with public-sector unions. The labor bosses instigated an invasion of the state capital with thousands of out-of-state protestors in an attempt to intimidate reformers from correcting the massive abuses that public- sector unions had caused.

The public saw through the propaganda and Governor Walker defeated the union attempt to recall him. He also won reelection for a second term and successfully put into place reforms that turned his state around, even in a bad economy. It is an inspiring story, showing that democracy can survive and thrive even in the face of mob rule, even in the face of a national campaign by the government-union money machine. That story would make a great movie. (See the book *Unintimidated: A Governor's Story and a Nation's Challenge* by Wisconsin Governor Scott Walker, 2013)

Union abuses are the reason why about half the states have enacted right to work laws. The reason for right to work laws is not an attempt to give non-union members an advantage over union members. The reason is to break up government sector labor monopolies. The reason is antitrust.

Those states who have right to work laws believe that monopolies, whether they be big business or big labor, must be restricted in order to keep the marketplace free. In the past, government employees—also known as public employees—were not permitted to unionize or go on strike. The good reasons for that policy in many cases have been forgotten or obscured by propaganda. Now we must re-learn the reason why. Even left-leaners such as President Franklin D. Roosevelt and union leader George Meany, head of the CIO, took positions against unionizing public employees. "It is impossible to bargain collectively with the government," said Meany. Roosevelt considered the prospect of public-sector unions as "unthinkable and intolerable."

The traditional unions, in times before the recent advent of government employee unions, were viewed as a vehicle to get workers some of the profits they helped create. Government workers, however, don't generate profits. The government is not a profit-making entity. Instead, it gets its money from the tax-payers. Government unions exercise their labor monopoly to negotiate for spending more tax money to pay their wages and pensions. When government unions strike, they strike against taxpayers (see "F.D.R. Warned Us," James Sherk, www.thefoundry.com, February 19, 2011).

Unionization, especially of government employees, can be itself a monopoly of the labor-force, an interference and denial of the free-market of labor. In many forms, it violates the same antitrust laws that broke up Standard Oil. Congress over the years, however, gave these unions special-interest exemptions from anti-monopoly laws ("Unions Exempt from Antitrust Law," *Wall Street Journal,* Feb. 27, 2011).

In 1935, when Congress granted unions many of the exemptions from the anti-trust law, the legislators didn't have in mind exempting unions of g*overnment employees.* The idea of a government union, itself, was generally unheard of at that time, especially in the view of President Franklin Roosevelt: ". . . Since their own services have to do with the functioning of the Government, a strike of public employees manifests nothing less than an intent on their part to prevent or obstruct the operations of Government until their demands are satisfied. Such action, looking toward the paralysis of Government by those who have sworn to support it, is unthinkable and intolerable."

In general, a closed shop allows only a union member to hold the job. In such cases, non-union workers cannot work. Closed shops generally use union dues to advance the political agenda of union *leaders,* regardless of the political philosophy of the dues-paying union *worker.* This is also true even of most open shops.

A substantial portion of governmental services—police and fire services, air traffic control, prison guards, public utilities, public hospitals and emergency facilities, public transportation systems, teachers—if they decided to strike would cripple the economy or endanger society.

But most significantly, collective bargaining between government workers and the government itself suffers from a raw conflict of interest. Government employee unions contribute hundreds of millions of dollars to the campaign coffers of their favorite politicians, who happen to be in a position to "earn their pay" by directly raising the employees' wages and benefits. And they do so on the backs of taxpayers. As a wise man once said, "Politics makes strange bedfellows rich."

Unions in the private sector, on the other hand, suffer from no such conflict of interest. Although they can and do contribute to politicians' election campaigns, the politicians are in no position to directly raise the wages and benefits of private sector employees. Unlike politicians, private sector employers must keep in mind—and protect—a profit margin for their company when they consider wage increases. On the other hand, when the politicians consider raising wages they can raise taxes, print more money, or rob from other public programs to pay off the unions.

Not only do governmental employees unions have a conflict of interest, they have a stronger tendency to feather their nests than do private sector employees. Because they and the politicians act under the public trust, their natural competitive instincts to favor or put their own self-interests ahead of that of the public is, itself, a conflict of interest.

For example, public unions tend to push for unnecessary or phantom programs just to give themselves soft jobs. Moreover, when unionized, they find themselves able to dictate to the politicians whom they financially helped elect—their bosses—the terms of their own nest-feathering, including salary raises and pensions."Taxpayers spent around $156 million on federal employees who did no federal work at all," said Nathan Mehrens, president of Americans for Limited Government." By Kenric Ward / August 11, 2014. "Watchdog.org reported 8-11-14 that union business—oxymoronically classified as "official time"—is subsidized by the IRS. Mehrens uncovered similar behavior at other agencies." By Kenric Ward.

In the private sector, however, the growth of wages, salaries, and benefits are naturally constrained by the market and reality:

the employer has to afford the raises. If not, he and the company will go broke (á la General Motors). In the public sector, on the other hand, bureaucrats have an arsenal of weapons with which to pay increases in wages and benefits.

The most common weapon is, of course, to raise taxes. I have others above. Such acts, of course, cause inflation and drain value from the public and from the savers.

Governmental employee unions and the symbiotic legislature are like the metaphoric foxes in the henhouse, a situation that places taxpayers at the mercy of the government and its employees. As said above, when public unions strike, they shut down essential services and hold the public hostage.

Look what has happened in California since government employees became legally able to strike. During Jerry Brown's first term as California governor many years ago, he signed the bill that gave public-sector unions the right to unionize and strike. (Those who argue that it was Democrat Grey Davis who signed the bill haven't offered proof of that to my satisfaction.) . This kicked open the government union floodgates all over the country.

We are reminded that government unions overwhelmingly finance the campaigns of pro-union politicians. As a result, the legislature in California is as of 2015 so lopsided that Democrats hold a super majority of more than two thirds of the legislature. Since gaining that power, the formerly "Golden State" of California has become grossly insolvent (at the time of writing this book), and industries are moving out.

The state unemployment rate was 9.8 % as of 2012, according to Aaron Sankin of the *Huffington Post*. California was previously tied with Rhode Island for the highest unemployment rate in the entire nation. It's sluggishly now moving upward as of 2015, but they de-emphasize in the reports the number of those who have given up looking for jobs, or who can't find a salary close to what they earned before, or who can't get a full time job. The national labor participation rate is now far worse than it was 8 years ago, while at the same time the population has increased . . . For these and other reasons, we have difficulty swallowing the latest hype on the so-called unemployment rate reduction.

According to Caroline May, writing for Breitbart on June 2, 2015, over 93,636 million people in the U.S. were not participating in the work force—the worst participation percentage/rate in 38 years. The real California unemployment rate as of 2013 was 14.6%. (Rick Sloan, *Union of Unemployed*, March 8, 2013) and had been over 14 percent for the prior three years. The state is in the stranglehold of powerful government unions that generate campaign funds for the very politicians who vote for those same bloated government employee salaries, benefits, and pension increases. Yet no one seems concerned. Where is the free press?

In the past, *civil service* laws were enacted for the benefit of government employees, primarily because government workers were not allowed to unionize. Under these laws, government employees were granted many extra protections, such as tenure and pensions, which generally were unavailable to private sector employees. But now government workers in many jurisdictions enjoy the benefits of *both* civil service laws *and* the power to unionize and strike.

From a co-opetition standpoint, the governmental employees' unions have over-competed and the state legislators have über-cooperated—i.e., been overly accommodating. The states caught in this dilemma are forced to raise taxes, as a result of which private-sector jobs are moving out. For example, compare the last several years of the level of growth of the economies of California and Texas. The difference is stark.

Even in 2014 California's jobless rate is still among the highest in the nation, while Texas' unemployment rate declined to 4.2 percent, one of the nation's lowest rates... Despite the state's job growth, 1.2 million of California's 18.9 million-worker labor force are still unemployed, while Texas has just 558,943 unemployed in its 13.1 million-worker labor pool. . . . Despite the state's job growth, 1.2 million of California's 18.9 million-worker labor force are still unemployed, while Texas has just 558,943 unemployed in its 13.1 million-worker labor pool. *Debate Raged,* by Ron Walters, Sacramento Bee, April 2015.

According to Yahoo Finance, July 2014, Part of the appeal of the Lone Star state, in addition to lower taxes, says CKE's outspoken chief executive, Andy Puzder, is that "you don't have the very burdensome wage and hour laws that you have in California."

The argument that Texas is more inherently endowed with oil and gas and natural resources than is the Golden State is nonsense. Both possess oil and some parts of NASA, but California also has aerospace/ aviation manufacturing, wine, the movie and TV industries, agriculture, and Silicon Valley, among a thousand other productive assets. Unfortunately it also has ultra-left-leaners who feel they are doing the right thing by influencing the voting public and unintentionally killing the goose that lays the golden egg.

That goose used to be golden California. Only a handful of years ago, the state ranked as one of the six strongest economies in the entire world, out-producing even the Western European country of Italy. At last count, it had dropped far below Italy to eighth place in the world and is still sinking.

In the past, government employees were referred to as "public servants" and were compensated on a scale slightly below that of workers with commensurate jobs in the private sector. The rationale was that government employees enjoyed more job security and superior benefits. Further, private employees generally produced more per hour than did government employees.

But in the thirty years or so since government employees were first allowed to go on strike, government salaries, benefits, and pensions have become at least 33 percent greater than equivalent compensation in the private sector. According to an April 10, 2010 article in *USA Today*, the pay gap between government workers and private workers is still growing, even in our distressed economy.

Federal figures show that, as of December 2008, public employees received extra benefits worth an average of $13.38 an hour, while private-sector workers got benefit worth only $7.98 an hour. The Bureau of Labor Statistics (BLS) says that overall, total compensation for state and local public workers was $39.25 an hour—$11.90 an hour more than workers in comparable jobs in the private sector.

The gap has been expanding because of the increasing value of public employee benefits. In 2012 alone, governmental benefits rose three times higher than those in the private sector: up sixty-nine cents an hour for civil servants, verses twenty-three cents for private workers.

As a result of this, approximately half of all state and local spending is consumed by labor costs according to BLS and census data. Benefits consume a growing share of that. To date, it constitutes 34 percent. I refer again to Governor Brown's first term of as governor of California when he reportedly opened Pandora's Box by signing the bill that changed the law to allow government employees to unionize and strike. Incredibly, government employee unions continue to receive by far the highest pay and benefits of equivalent jobs anywhere in the world.

If it were in present day California, it's possible the California prison guard Sluggo in *The Tortoise Shell Game* could have made over $150,000 in 2013, including overtime and accumulated vacation pay. "G" unions have become so powerful they turned former governor Arnold Schwarzenegger from the financial hero for California he touted himself to be to the man sitting at the head table of the banquet that ran his state into insolvency.

Too much cooperation with public sector labor by the Democrat-run California legislature, exacerbated by too little competition by the voters and taxpayers of the state have led to California's current condition.

Importance of Secret Ballot

With many unions there is no such thing as a secret ballot for its members. The shop bosses have various means of finding out how the members voted. With regard to the issue of voting in general, in a democratic society, many would-be influential people—and ordinary people, for that matter—are afraid to say in public what they believe in private—what they believe in their hearts. Some of the reasons for their reticence are: protect their jobs, their families, their companies, their businesses , their relations with regulators, their place in the neighborhood, their survival in the next election if they are politicians—protection from intimidation and retribution. Thus, when a potential voter has to register and reveal , for example: what party he belongs to, or whether he voted consistently with the wishes of a union boss, or to whom he contributed campaign funds, he understandably might be reluctant to reveal his true beliefs. Otherwise, he could become the victim of intimidation, as happened with the IRS scandal of targeting certain groups seeking tax exemptions during 2013-2014. I suspect—as in the case of the Kate Steimle murder in San Francisco, which resulted from a Sanctuary City policy—that many politicians in those cities are afraid to speak up against the special interests that got them elected. I suspect that some of those politicians would privately welcome the voice of a courageous soul who would speak up and change public opinion and thus save the politician from being booted out of office for expressing his true feelings. In the coopetition equation the courageous voice is illustrative of *competition*; the Political Correction and Sanctuary City policy is illustrative of *naive or forced-cooperation*. Labor laws that exempt unions from anti-monopoly regulation should at least require a secret ballot for their members.

EXCESSIVE CEO SALARIES
AND GOLDEN PARACHUTES

As examples of seeming failures of capitalism, liberals delight in pointing to the supposedly excessive salaries and pension packages of some U.S. public company chief executives. (They are silent, of course, on the astronomical salaries of super athletes, super movie and TV stars, and rich liberals in general.)

Jack Welch, when he was CEO of General Electric, was one of the first of those corporate magnates to begin such practice of being favored with extraordinary personal benefits; a multitude of others have followed. In 2008, the news that Carly Fiorina, former CEO of Hewlett Packard, and Meg Whitman, former CEO of eBay, had each taken enormous golden-parachute bonus packages no doubt unfairly contributed to their unsuccessful ventures into politics.

The so-called excessive salary/golden parachute story unjustly damages the image of capitalism and gives support to leftist ideas. At this time in the U.S., conservatives believe they cannot afford further erosion of support. A fair explanation is in order. Less well-known is the fact that Welch's replacement at GE, Jeffery Immelt, several years ago waived—voluntarily—a huge part of his compensation package. Perhaps he was thinking of running for something, so in preparation did he do a bit of landscaping?

Of course, when a company is a private enterprise and the CEO has enough share-control, or if he/she convinces in good faith that he/she is worth the compensation package in question, nothing—especially prospective government regulation—should stand in the way of the parachute popping open. I will give the benefit of the doubt to Fiorina, and Whitman as having in good faith earned their compensation. Papers filed in Welch's divorce perhaps raised some issues.

However, if the CEO holds control by illegitimate means, or if the shareholders are denied fair democratic representation on the board of directors, the case is different. Ironically, when you analyze why abuse happens, you find that usually the failure is caused by too much cooperation rather than from the competition side of capitalism.

Consider that, if you held substantial shares in a company, would you tolerate its board of directors—which is supposed to act on your behalf—giving excessive salary and pension packages to its CEOs? Of course not; your self-interest is to increase profits and reduce costs. Then how does unconscionably massive compensation occur? Simple: because instead of acting on your behalf, some boards are in the pockets of their CEOs.

On the subject of excessive executive compensation, the needle is at about two o'clock in the U.S. It should be at about noon. However, the reconciliation should be accomplished without the force of government, except to ensure that by law corporate charters and bylaws are kept truly democratic—that is, a bill of rights should exist for shareholders.

Here's one of the ways abuses like excessive salary situations came to pass. About forty years ago, some influential "altruists" had the idea that some of the members of public-company boards of directors should be laypersons—non-shareholder-outsiders. The rationale was that such outsiders would give "fairer" consideration to social issues, such as to the environment and social justice, as opposed to straight profit for the company.

At first blush, this makes sense. After all, non-shareholder board appointees would not have the self-interest about profits that shareholder members do. But when making decisions about, for instance, executive compensation, non-shareholder board members are more apt to look the other way if they can trade-off a little "social justice" benefit in exchange for giving the CEO an excessive salary. By "social justice," I mean here, for example, uber-consideration to the environment, union benefits, minimum wage, immigration, and health care issues and so on.

Do you see the unintended consequence of such thinking? The CEO simply hand-picks or heavily influences the picks of his or her outside directors, then turns them into unwitting or willing pawns.

I suspect that something more is happening under the proverbial board table. Imagine this hypothetical scenario: an employees' union acquires such a huge block of its company's shares that it places its own man on the board. Soon this union-elected board member and the company CEO realize that the situation can serve each of them well, and they consider scratching each other's backs. In exchange for better benefits for union workers, the board member will vote for a better than usual salary package for the CEO—even if this quid pro quo is detrimental to the company as a whole.

What's wrong with that? It is bribery and corruption, that's what is wrong with it. It puts the self-interest of the CEO above his legally binding fiduciary duties to the company.

What should be done to prevent this? The rights of shareholders of listed public companies should be guaranteed by a "shareholder's bill of rights" built into the Articles of Incorporation and bylaws of the company. In this document, conflicts of interest should be strictly banned, and all directors should have the self-interest of either owning substantial shares of the company or of representing blocks of its shareholders.

Furthermore, the chairman of the board and the chief executive of the public company should never be the same person. Why not? Because it's a conflict of interest. The CEO manages the company. The chairman represents the board to be sure that the CEO is doing his job. If not, the chairman should be looking for talent to replace the CEO. Do you think the CEO will normally be on the lookout for his own replacement? I don't think so.

All directors should be elected by the shareholders. The supposed altruistic policy of appointing directors without self-interest should be banned.

Approximately forty years ago, all directors to the California State Bar Association were required to be members of the bar. Someone later convinced the bar to allow members of the public to serve on a few seats of the board. Supported by the votes of these new laypersons, the bar soon opened the practice of law to what some regard as the distasteful, unprofessional commercialism of the of the profession: advertising.

Most regard marketing as a form of freedom of speech, but

there are those who believe it turns a profession into a business. Again, we see the cooperation/ accommodation of allowing advertising versus the competition/ protectionism of professionalism. Is the latter really a form of protectionism? Does advertising benefit the client in terms of lowering fees? I do not see evidence of it.

PRICE FIXING AND CARTELS

Price fixing is a form of co-opetition, which happens to be illegal, generally. It is a restraint of free competition, free-enterprise; it is a form of group monopoly. It is a violation of the coopetition synthesis; there is too much competition by the price-fixing associates and not enough cooperation with the consumers. The price fixers cooperate among themselves to take advantage (compete with) the best interests of the consumers.

14

A Piece of the
Capitalist Pie and More
Issues of Political Science

To properly grow the economy, the policy of the government should be to place the point of ultimate synthesis—the sweet spot—at about 1:30 on the scale. Government action should not interfere with anyone's opportunity, if he so desires, to grab a piece of the capitalist pie. By that I mean that after taxes, the tax-payer should be left *some* money, however small the amount, to invest in the capitalist pie. And the more money the government doesn't tax away, the greater the investment that can be made by the taxpayer and the greater his piece of the capitalist pie.

In general, therefore, the greater the investments from the public, the faster the economy grows. The faster the economic growth, the more people that are able to invest, and all ships begin to rise on the economic sea.

For example, a person left with only five percent of every dollar he or she earns is unlikely to invest in higher-risk-return ventures. Instead, if prudent, he might make investments that tend toward less rapid growth. However, a person left with 75 percent of each dollar is more likely to invest in riskier ventures, new inventions or things that tend to grow the economy at a faster rate.

After an ordinary family or a single person pays for reasonable and necessary living expenses, college education costs, taxes, and makes modest entertainment and vacation expenditures, enough should be left for the family or individual to invest some money in the capitalist pie. That should be government policy.

The important reason for this is that increasing longevity requires everyone to set aside sufficient funds for decent living at old age. Concomitantly, because increased private investment makes the economy grow, more people are put to work and kept working; they all benefit. This is a win-win; this is synergy; this is mother nature and capitalism at work. This is co-opetition.

If we calculate the amount of funds necessary for a meaningful middle-income life, the picture begins to sharpen. Let us take into consideration the inevitable unexpected costs that occur in anyone's life: health problems, business reversals, casualty losses, natural disasters, crime losses, divorce, unemployment, the deaths or injuries of loved ones, any number of unexpected events, including the effects of alcohol or drugs. Many of these problems seem to come out of nowhere, and almost everyone experiences one or more of them.

In America, after the middle-income family or individual deducts from its/his gross income almost 50 percent for the aggregate of federal, state, sales, and local taxes, there remains insufficient money for investment in the capitalist pie or, for that matter, to build any kind of nest-egg for senior life. Part of the problem is obvious: a substantial portion of those taxes pay for wasteful or bloated government bureaucracies. Shame on politicians, special interests, and the media for being oblivious to the problem.

Jimmy Fallon quipped: "The President said the federal government can no longer spend taxpayers' money like it is Monopoly money. Especially since Monopoly money is now more valuable than the dollar."

Keep the good programs, but streamline and trim those that are wasteful or obsolete. How does one determine which programs are "good?" Most can be identified with a little logic and reasoning using the co-opetition scale. The rest must be haggled out by ordinary political machinations.

With lower taxes, people will retain more cash for acquiring a piece of the capitalist pie. Therefore, we should shift the fulcrum to emphasize natural competition for personal and family financial advancement rather than attempting income redistribution. We should shift to emphasize income *generation*, allowing the unproductive to become productive so they gain a piece of the pie. The byproduct for everyone would be a stronger economy, which, in turn, raises all ships—especially the ghost ship of the unemployed.

THE ASSOCIATION OF PRODUCTIVE AMERICANS

Perhaps productive citizens—the largely unrepresented middle-income workers who are so close to the fulcrum—should themselves become activists and form their own lobby in order to compete against the special interests for a piece of the pie. In that way, they may serve to bring a better synthesis to the equation. As it is, many argue that their middle-income voices in the

U.S. are drowned out by those of special interests on both the far left and far right.

Some say the AARP, for example, often supports policies in conflict with the best interests of its members. Its tax exempt status has been challenged (*Behind the Veil—The AARP America Doesn't Know*, Wally Herger and Dave Reichert of the U.S. House Ways and Means Committee, 2011).

The voices of the inadequately-represented middle class are further drowned out by teachers' unions, other government-sector unions, and lobbies for bureaucracies, multinational corporations, and others. Rather than pursuing campaign reform to reduce the influence of lobbyists, I suggest that these underrepresented middle-income multitudes compete by organizing and doing their own lobbying. Such a group, with its many millions of potential members, would be very powerful indeed. Such an organization could be named something like the Association of Productive Americans (A.P.A.).

Much campaign reform was declared unconstitutional anyway (*Citizens United v. Federal Election Commission*, 558 U.S. (2010), and, if carefully analyzed, the Campaign Reform Act erodes freedom of speech. The First Amendment allows one to pay for and use a megaphone, a sound truck or an advertising agency, among others, to promote a position. It is called free speech.

NO TOLERANCE FOR CONFLICTS OF INTEREST

Compete! Don't ask for more government control or more über-cooperation, except to abolish all circumstances of conflict of interest. Perhaps an A.P.A. (Association of Productive Americans) could seek to enact laws preventing government bureaucracies or their unions from lobbying on issues in which they possess conflicts of interest.

When a government bureaucracy takes a *political* position on programs affecting the general public and that position coincidentally also benefits the bureaucracy it suffers a serious conflict of interest. This is so, unless its position is against its self-interest. For example, if it advocates ending the life of its bureaucracy, that would not constitute a conflict of interest.

Any government agency should always be nonpolitical. Yes, the bureaucracy should continue to render reports and present facts, and it might even advocate the benefits of its programs—but never when doing so also promotes its self-interest. The practice of government bureaucracies' contributing or fund-raising, either directly or indirectly, to political campaigns relating to their bureaucracy should be banned.

The practice of privately lobbying legislators in cases where the bureaucracy or its members are acting under a conflict of interest (i.e., promoting self-interested matters outside the public hearing venue) should also be banned. And in cases where the government does promote programs by way of public hearing, they should disclose any color of conflict of interest as part of their presentation. The cliché, "Don't let the fox guard the henhouse" will never lose its validity.

By way of example, some argue that the decline in educational proficiency in the U.S. is related to influence of teachers' unions (not teachers individually) because the unions promulgate ineffective educational programs while laboring under conflicts of interest. The argument is that the unions were more interested in preserving jobs and salaries for teachers than they were in helping provide good education for students.

Although educators should by all means be free to argue and present their cases before local school boards, perhaps the local constituency should carefully weigh the merits of placing educational administrators directly on their school boards. In those circumstances almost any administrator would labor under built-in conflicts of interest.

Bureaucrats, quasi-government, and government employees have inherent conflicts of interest. The others—the non-government groups—do not. Although the Constitution rightfully does not allow the curtailment of freedom of speech for those without conflicts of interest; the courts have properly upheld restrictions against those having conflicts of interest. (The U.S. Supreme Court ruled 9–0 that ethics laws on conflict of interest did not violate the free speech, First Amendment Rights of a legislator: *Nevada Commission on Ethics v Corrigan*, June 5, 2011.)

AVOIDING POLITICAL POLARIZATION—WITHOUT COMPROMISING GOOD FAITH PRINCIPLES

Is it possible for a U.S. Congressman or Senator to avoid polarization and still adhere to his or her good faith principles? I think so, if the representative cooperates even as he or she competes regarding the issue under consideration. They would cooperate by always presenting their arguments in good faith, rationally, and civilly; they'd also argue without resorting to criminality, deceit, trickery, or falsehood—and do so even without gross exaggeration. Yet at the same time, they'd compete by sticking to their guns on their rational, good-faith principles.

What do I mean by *good faith*? It means acting without deception. It means not to allow the ends to justify the means.

This technique of cooperating while competing is, of course, co-opetition. To use this technique does not mean legislators can't argue a position vociferously and with great passion, especially when it is in the rational self-interest of their constituency. It's just that the legislator should always act within the rules of civility.

There need not be witless compromise just for the sake of compromise. If for some reason the most rational position does not prevail, the fact of such a failure is the best evidence that during the course of negotiation someone broke the rules—someone failed to act in good faith.

Abiding by these rules would enable everyone to more quickly resolve issues; if everyone acts in good faith, there is much greater likelihood that the most rational positions will eventually prevail. But how do we know when legislators break the rules? We know when we see them acting irrationally or in bad faith. We are alerted further when we see them resort to trickery, exaggeration, fraud, bluster, deceit, or criminality, or when we discern they believe the ends justify the means.

The ends justifying the means is based on the belief that, for example, it is okay to deceive if doing so achieves a result the deceiver thinks is good. For example, a belief that it's okay to lie to the public about what a proposed law means if you think the law would be good for the public.

Such extreme competition—attempting to achieve a particular end by taking a devious low road—is, a favorite tool of despots and dictators. It leads to polarization rather than to its avoidance.

Polar rigidity is also exacerbated when special interests seek political power or financial gain ahead of the best interests of their constituencies or their country. For, as a wise person once said, when buying and selling are controlled by legislators, the first things to be bought and sold are legislators.

Polarization may also occur, albeit unintentionally, when the representative suffers from irrational bias, cultism/brainwashing, mental illness, incompetency, or from the influence of drugs or chemicals.

Moreover, a prejudiced, non-objective, or lazy press and media that misinforms the representative or his/her constituency can also drive polarization. Typically, this happens if the media compounds the problem by manipulating the news and politicizing its own particular agenda. For example, in the Trayvon Martin tragedy, one of the major networks deliberately cut and pasted parts of the 911 call made by George Zimmerman to make it seem like Mr Zimmerman had made racist statements.

However, one overriding question about polarization must be asked. Should such rigidity be avoided in *all* cases—? even at the expense of giving up one's good faith principles? The answer is a resounding *no*. During negotiations, when one side breaks the rules, we shouldn't turn the other cheek and give up our rational principles in compromise. The common law, since the time of Rome and Phoenicia, dealing with that problem has evolved over thousands of years. Generally, in law the first side to break a condition precedent breaches the contract and excuses the other side from complying with his or her remaining conditions.

In such circumstances, the gloves should come off. The American Revolution, the Declaration of Independence of July 4th, 1776, the U.S Constitution and its Amendments all exemplify "taking off the gloves" to preserve the good faith principles. The founders instituted separation of powers partly to encourage us to sometimes fight it out—to polarize—so no one would gain total power.

The first party resorting to bad faith, fraud, deceit, and totalitarianism, excuses the others from trusting the dialectic process. In such cases, a continuing state of polarity is better than witless capitulation or compromise against one's good faith principles.

(Note: rational self-interest should not be confused with conflict of interest. Where an advocate is a fiduciary or trustee for a beneficiary, he cannot take a position against the best interests of his fiduciary-beneficiary. To do so is a conflict of interest.)

IMPORTANT DIFFERENCES BETWEEN GOVERNMENT–AFFILIATED LOBBYISTS AND NON-GOVERNMENT AFFILIATED LOBBYISTS

There is a popular argument that we shouldn't pick on bureaucrats or government-employee-special interests because there are *other* special interest groups, such as big corporations and non-government-employee unions, who also exercise power. This argument is flawed. There is a difference among government-affiliated groups and the others: government-affiliated groups and quasi-government agencies must serve the public trust as a first priority.

WHAT IS SO BAD ABOUT THE GOVERNMENT RAISING TAXES OR ENGAGING IN IMPROVIDENT BORROWING DURING A PERSISTENT RECESSION?

The answer to this question is simple, and we've partially answered it before. Raising taxes during a recession drains away valuable private capital that should remain available for investment in private enterprise and, thus, into the economy; the tax drain results in bad economic consequences. As noted, excessive taxing is *forced or über-cooperation*, whereas accumulating capital is a form of *competition*.

To get the economy going and keep it going, it is absolutely necessary that sufficient capital from private investors—private capital—remains available for investment in private enterprise. This includes funds from Wall Street. By "private capital" I mean any funds that do not come from the government.

In the vast majority of cases, two sources of funds make up the components of financing a typical private-enterprise project. They are: (i) the investment of equity capital, and (ii) the lending of debt funds. The typical ratio of investment of equity capital to debt funds for any single financing transaction is, more or less, one-third equity investment to two-thirds loan. Such equity investments are generally more high-risk, and for the most part only the rich or Wall Street-capital pools can afford this adventure-travel with such perils. Only *they* have the surplus funds at hand for those purposes.

On high risk projects, the lenders will not fund a loan unless the required proportion of private investment capital is already in or is concurrently coming into the project. By that I mean that the potential borrower needs to "show the money"—the availability of it—to the lender. The "show me the money" aphorism became famous from the movies: Jay Leno once said: "And Blagojevich held a press conference. Did you see his press conference? I love this. He quoted the British poet Tennyson. He quoted Tennyson, which was weird, because usually he quotes the movie 'Jerry Maguire.' 'Show me the money!'"

So what happens when those surplus funds in the hands of potential investors are taxed? It takes the funds out of the pool of potential sources for investment. If too much is taken, the economy stops moving. Building stops. Business and manufacturing are stunted. The nation goes into deeper recession or is kept in recession. Or the outrigged pontoon has become too fat and heavy and the canoe wallows in the sea.

Moreover, if the government goes too much into debt during a recession, it has to increase its borrowings to pay back the principal and interest on the debt, which compounds the problem. U.S. Treasury bonds and notes are examples. To sell the bonds, the government has to make them very attractive to investors. The government, therefore, finds itself going into competition for private-capital funds, which would otherwise be available for private-enterprise projects. The government competes against private entrepreneurs who also look to the same pool of investment money.

To attract people willing to buy government securities, the U.S. Treasury finds itself increasing the interest rate it is willing to pay to bond buyers. The result of this pressure on the supply and demand of private capital is that the government sucks those funds from the marketplace—funds that would otherwise be available to entrepreneurs.

In this scenario, not only is an entrepreneur cut off from his supply of investment capital, but the impact on the economy is compounded by the battering ram of government debt piled on top of excessive taxation. How much government taxation and borrowing is "excessive?" The answer is any amount that may impose a dampening effect on the economy; any amount that might slow the economy; any amount that the government will have to scramble (e.g. print more money or raise taxes) to pay back; or, metaphorically, any amount that could fatten the pontoon and cause the outrigger canoe to slow down and wallow in the sea.

In *The Tortoise Shell Game*, as Anthony's escape boat wallows in the sea while fleeing Bramoso's gun boats, he laments that they were not sailing an outrigger canoe—the symbol of a good economy. Thus, a government must learn to err on the side of caution. The Great Recession of 2008, which is continuing at this writing in California and other States teaches us that the unintended consequences are too great to justify the government taking chances and raising taxes. I remind us of the debacle in 2008, when the bursting of the subprime mortgage bubble fire-hosed the private investors down the drain.

These investors will not likely re-invest in the economy until the government reduces its borrowing and taxation and refrains from more ill-conceived social engineering. At this writing, the clock scale is at about 11:00 (excessive cooperation). It needs to be at about 1:15 (more competition from the private entrepreneur).

To help instill confidence in the future, it is time for a U.S. balanced budget amendment. Approximately thirty-eight states have one, and Canada is reemerging economically, many believe, much because of its recent balanced budget policies.

TOO MUCH GROWTH IS ALSO SOMETIMES BAD

Gregory Bateson's, the anthropologist, declared that in nature, governing loops will sooner or later rise to cut back on most types of exponential growth. The governing loop is a form of nature's cooperation, reducing excessive competition—bringing some order to chaotic growth. On our co-opetition clock scale, population control should be at around 12:15 p.m. Alarmingly, I place it now at approximately 2:45.

Many years ago while vacationing in Acapulco, Mexico, I was drawn by the sound of loudspeakers to a back-city square where thousands of local people were celebrating an event of some sort. I soon learned they were giving the Father of the Year Award that day. A proud older man filed his way through tumultuous applause to the stage in the center of the huge crowd. That winner had fathered twenty-six children—and that accomplishment, together with being poor, was why he'd won.

The population of the earth is rising exponentially. We don't need experts like Paul Ehrlich, Matthew Connelly, or Robert

Engelmann to expound any further on that. We know. the evidence is there. Largely because of growing populations, the earth is fast running out of fresh water—drinking water and potable water for farming.

Most, if not all of the earth's water came to us from comets and meteors that impacted our planet in primordial times. We received a finite supply, and of that, non-potable ocean water comprises ninety-nine percent of the total.

There is no question that overpopulation now seriously impacts the planet's environment. We see it all around us. Only a few months ago, I visited the Galapagos Islands of Ecuador and saw firsthand the struggle to preserve them. The biggest battle raged between the islander-Ecuadorians and the throngs of their countrymen on mainland Ecuador. Intrastate migration of Ecuadoreans to their Islands is limited to practically zero. For environmental reasons, only a limited number of residents are allowed to live on the Galapagos Islands, irrespective of whether they be Ecuadorian citizens.

To supply the needs and fancies of the growth of populations around the Globe we are compelled to do things that could harm ourselves in particular and our blue planet in general. One of many examples is, of course, our use plastic packaging as one method of preserving and extending the shelf-life of our food. But debates rage not only over the fossil fuel plastic it is made of, but over whether those plastics might cause cancer. Called into question are biphenyl A (BPA), polyvinyl chloride (PVC), and diethylhexyl phthalate (DEHP) (But see "Microwaves and Plastic Containers," The Canadian Cancer Society, March 11, 2011).

Education is a huge factor in the voluntary control of population growth. On the one hand, while laws limiting growth appear to go against nature, they have proven somewhat effective in

China. To some extent, that must be due to voluntary cooperation, although we also know of government imposed, forced-cooperation. Now, however, that country is faced with an unforeseen consequence: the male-child-Little-Emperor syndrome. In China, among these single male children, many are becoming obese and have a strong sense of entitlement.

Someday biochemists will figure out how to preselect sperm without violating the teachings of the various religions or of nature, and in this way make headway on the overpopulation problem. More importantly, history has shown that in various dominions, when the population reaches a critical point, nature kicks in a governing loop in which there is a voluntary low-to-zero population growth . Again, we see cooperation occurring naturally to reduce the competition of excessive childbirth. Examples would be what's happening in east Asia and eastern Europe. There, populations are shrinking.

If growth is guided, not forced or mandated, to a rate symbolized by 12:15 p.m. on our co-opetition scale, eventually the human population of earth should stabilize. I believe that nature's intuitive goal will leave enough growth to override natural attrition, but allow the earth to end up with zero population growth.

A UN study predicted that Earth in 2300 will stabilize at nine billion people (see "World Population in 2300 Could Stabilize at 9 Billion, UN Estimates," *UN News Centre*, November 4, 2004). Others predict it will end up at eleven billion people. At this Printing, it is at about seven billion.

In the 1960s, ethologist John B. Calhoun did experiments with rats, revealing the effects of over-crowding. He referred to it as Behavior Sink. The population would grow to a point where expansion would cease and then fall back. The society would break down, often violently, and the rats would not reproduce. Often they'd become cannibalistic. Finally a less crowded equilibrium would result. Perhaps a parallel scenario might befall the human species. A governing loop would arise from nature.

In any event, a phenomenon of increasing longevity throws a monkey-wrench into this scenario. That could be the subject of a whole new book. In the final analysis, though, a combination of our minds, ingenuity, and Gregory Bateson's natural governing loop, without government injunctions, may very well solve the problem, which will concomitantly ameliorate the environmental problems, and—as I say, naturally, peacefully and for free.

Nuclear Weapon Proliferation; the U.S. Has the Obligation to Prevent It At All Costs. In 1945, near the end of the Second World War, the military experts estimated that perhaps 200,000 more U.S. troops would lose their lives if the allies were forced to invade the Japanese mainland. The U.S. had spent 23 billion dollars secretly developing the Atomic Bomb. After warning the Japanese that a calamitous new weapon would be unleashed against them if they did not unconditionally surrender, President Truman finally authorized dropping the Atomic Bomb. Two successive bombs destroyed the Japanese cities of Nagasaki and Hiroshima.

At that time the huge benefit to the allies was, of course, the ending of the war. The huge detriment was, among other things, the birth and unleashing upon the earth of an abominable weapon of mass destruction. In hoped-for partial mitigation of that dreary result, in 1970 America signed the Nuclear Non-Proliferation treaty. From the very beginning of the development of the bomb the U.S. had a sacred, moral duty and possibly even a legal obligation to prevent the proliferation of that technology or the availability of enriched atomic materials. Sadly

America failed to fulfill this duty. The U.S. negligently or naively allowed the proliferation of its Frankenstein's child. It therefore has the duty and obligation to stop any further spreading, even to draw back the proliferation wherever possible.

It is now well known that spies were at work even before the first bomb was dropped. The government sent the Rosenberg couple to death for their crimes of espionage, but the secret had already gotten into the hands of the Soviet Union. The Soviets gave certain spy-gained technology to China. In 1951 Peking signed a secret agreement with Moscow through which China provided uranium ores in exchange for Soviet assistance in the nuclear field. In mid-October 1957 the Chinese and Soviets signed an agreement on new technology for national defense that included a provision for additional Soviet nuclear assistance.

Other countries, including Israel, also got the technology by spying on the U.S. In Pakistan's case, the U.S. negligently –some would argue—intentionally, handed critical technology to the Pakistanis, who then sold it to North Korea, and Iran. The Pakistanis could not have afforded to spend their own 23 billion to develop the bomb. They bought it for far less. (Generally, see The Man Who Knew Too Much, by Adrian Levy and Cathy-Scott Clark, The Guardian, October 13, 2007.)

The U. S. wanted Pakistan's help in dealing with Afghanistan. The story is about former CIA agent Rich Barlow who blew the whistle on the U. S. government. He had to sue for his pension. The U.S. eventually gave him a promise of a 1million dollar settlement for his lost pension claim, but there is a serious question of whether the government ever released the money to him.

Here is the important part to this proliferation issue. The U.S. has the duty to prevent Iran from obtaining nuclear weapons. It has the duty to police the earth to prevent any other nation or person from manufacturing the very expensive enriched weapons-grade materials necessary to make them. It has the duty to recover from all others that nuclear weapon capability. It can still do so by the use of treaties, sanctions, and economic influence.

Coopetition comes into play: Unleashing the technology was competition. Controlling the monster is cooperation or forced cooperation—cooperation with most of the people of the earth who have no chance against those who have that weapon.

15

Productive Disparity Between People, and the Ultimate Synthesis

This is the subject of productive disparity—I.e. between those who able to, and do, sustain themselves, and those who are not able to, and/ or do not, sustain themselves.

Here I believe we are woefully low on our ultimate synthesis scale. Fewer and fewer productive people are capable of carrying the load necessary to sustain both themselves and the remaining non-productive people. A number of people carrying the load for others is a big part of Marx's dogma. Redistribute from the capable to the incapable, from the young to the old, from the healthy to the ill, from the haves to the have-nots, from the productive to the unproductive.

When it happens spontaneously through altruism, empathy, family responsibility and goodness of heart, it is a testament to the humanity of humankind. However when it is forced through government mandate, it is testimony to the tyranny that can envelop humankind. And this government mandate floats on the assumption that such a redistribution scheme works. It does not. It never did, and it never will; it is against nature and co-opetition.

I place the existing fulcrum at a woeful 10:30, when it should be brought to at least 2:30. Here's why:

The human evolved into today's species partly because of extreme competition; that is, the survival of the fittest. However, cooperation dating from prehistoric times was also a necessary aspect of survival. Why do you think we smile? The big reason is that we intuitively wish to attract team mates who can help us survive. Humans evolved with the behavioral urge to travel a line of synthesis between both the extreme tracks.

Today, however, we live in a protective bubble. Thanks to great advances in technology, medicine, food production, and shelter, the human species now threatens to overpopulate and pollute the earth like a cancer. The potential hazards from biological, chemical, or nuclear warfare are too horrendous even to contemplate. Humanity is way past the threshold of wiping out many other forms of life—perhaps including itself. If left unchecked, it is not beyond the realm of probability that human growth or some aberrant seed thereof may eventually entirely destroy its host, the earth.

Moreover, terrorists and despots have discovered advanced technology and are using it to extort and exact gain from others—even governments. They threaten heinous crimes, such as suicide bombings, mass-transportation hijackings, chemical and germ warfare, beheadings, or nuclear extermination.

With the advent and proliferation of ever-higher technology in the instruments of war, such dangers may worsen to the point where just a few weapons in the hands of terrorists can threaten entire populations. In fact, we are already there.

Peaceful countries must stay vigilant in the face of terrorist groups and rogue nations. Peace-loving nations would be wise to maintain the synthesis between good and evil by remaining militarily strong and continuing to develop state-of-the-art, technologically advanced, strategic defense systems. To assume that the many billions of people on earth can be all taught, or forced, or persuaded to live together without conflict would be absurd.

Sure, we might successfully persuade *most* of the people, but not all of them. There are some individuals, or even despotic leaders, who would blow up the entire world to attain a perceived paradise elsewhere—with perhaps a multitude of virgins, or perhaps fly on a UFO, trailing a comet. Seeking to trail a comet happened in 1996 with the 39 member-suicide of the Heaven's Gate cult in a Rancho Santa Fe mansion in a suburb of San Diego.

What's more, would you trust a radicalized so-called Islamist suicide-bomber, or any radical, for that matter, claiming to be of any particular religious persuasion or cult, whether Christian, Buddhist, atheist or otherwise, who will commit suicide to make a point? Would you trust him with a weapon of mass destruction?

The U.S. developed the nuclear bomb, which forced the end of the Second World War. A byproduct of that invention was the unleashing upon the earth of Frankenstein's babies—the proliferation of nuclear weapons of mass destruction. The U.S. had a moral duty to humankind to control and restrict such propagation. The U.S. failed to adequately execute its duty. Spying by foreign powers, negligence of the U.S. and naivety of its leaders were responsible. Under no circumstances should the U.S. allow further nuclear weapon proliferation to any country, including Iran. Moreover, it has the moral obligation to actively seek to retrench and de-weaponize nuclear arms where ever they may exist on earth, even with allies to the U.S.

Genetic deformations that result from the proliferation of mutations that could not survive but for new technologies in medicine contribute to devolution, or reverse evolution. On the other hand, environmental toxins, carcinogens, pesticides, HIV, and a myriad other agents at war with human life no doubt affect evolution as well.

Given all this, the relative capabilities among humans for healthful and productive living and survivability in the future could come into ever-greater disparity. In that case, greater and greater proportions of the population would become dependent upon a shrinking pool of productive individuals. Without a doubt, an increasingly greater ratio of people are falling into the "aged" category. Sooner or later, the capacity of the producers will become overly strained or even exhausted under this burden, resulting in tremendous economic and social upheaval. With a resounding ringing bell, this brings us to the next subject—Social Security.

SOCIAL SECURITY

We've discussed much about Social Security as a prelude to this final chapter on the subject. The old-age security requirements of those people in the U.S. lucky or prudent enough to have positioned themselves to receive private pension benefits are largely satisfied. However, the majority of the working public has no retirement plan to live on apart from the inadequate stipend they will receive from Social Security.

On this topic our ultimate synthesis scale is currently at 10:30 and should be moved to 1:00. It is clogged by an excess of forced cooperation and a dearth of competition. Co-opetition on this issue has never been allowed to prevail, so the system is inevitably going broke.

PUBLIC FINANCE (INVESTMENTS) RATHER THAN REDISTRIBUTION

In the long run, an answer to this dilemma is to give everyone the opportunity to grab a piece of the capitalist pie rather than attempting to transfer income from achievers to non-achievers. Give everyone a chance through a system of Invested Universal Social Security funding. Let the pie grow bigger, and there will be more slices.

What is more natural? Forced-cooperation through redistribution, or financing Social Security (including medical security) through investment in the natural workings of free enterprise and capitalism? Please note that I use the phrase "*finance* social security." In the U.S. we don't presently finance either social or medical security: we re-distribute. We take from one and give to another, which is a Ponzi scheme.

It's contrary to the idea of the 5th and 14th amendments of the U.S. Constitution—a government taking without fair compensation, and government discrimination among groups of people. It's a Marxist idea: "From each according to his ability, to each according to his needs."

WE GOT OFF ON THE WRONG FOOT

Contrary to common belief, the New Deal of Franklin D. Roosevelt and the Great Society of Lyndon Johnson—the parts that were primarily concepts of redistribution—were failures. The

Great Depression was prolonged for ten years because of ill-conceived policies—as will be shown below.

Examine the inner city today: far more failures than successes. People who could afford to leave inner cities did so, leaving the poor. Public Housing was an utter failure. The family unit has declined. It now takes two working parents rather than one to raise a family. Out-of-wedlock births have skyrocketed. An authoritarian approach, treating the inner city like an occupied territory, has resulted. More African Americans than ever are unemployed, especially the young and young adults. The fathers of black youths, poor whites, and other minorities, and whites in general, have abandoned their children and their wives and mates in great numbers. They've done so, in part, because government policies foster this behavior by picking up the slack—effectively letting the errant father off the hook.

Has the status of African-Americans improved? Federal bureaucratization of schools shows little improvement of education results. Poverty levels remain almost unchanged, even though proportionally more and more tax dollars are being spent. Thanks to the current administration, we are back to a system of "more welfare than workfare"—workfare being the shining accomplishment of President Bill Clinton, prodded by his Republican Congress of yesteryear.

We've forgotten that the welfare state turns citizens into clients and dependents. Between 2009 and 2012 the proportion of the public on food stamps is 20%, a rise of 44 percent thanks to underemployment and income stagnation (NBC Business News, Jeff Cox, 9-5- 2012). As of September 2013, the proportion of people working part-time jobs as opposed to working full-time jobs had increased dramatically.

Moreover, according to Gallup, the U.S. payroll-to population employment rate, or the percentage of adult Americans working full-time for an employer, fell to 43.7% in August of 2013, down from 44.6% in July and from 45.3% of the previous year (*House-Wire*, Jenny Marlar, 9-5-2013).

The national debt was about 10 trillion dollars when G.W. Bush left office. As of December 2013, it was over 17 trillion—a 70 percent increase in five years. Meanwhile the proportion spent on national defense has been severely cut while health care costs have exploded. Far fewer people have full-time jobs than five years earlier, yet the population of the country has increased. Government has demonstrated its inherent inability to control waste, fraud, and choking regulation.

HOW TO FINANCE SOCIAL SECURITY
AND MEDICAL SECURITY

Truly *finance* it. Don't try to redistribute it. The politicians and economists were all wrong in the 1930s; they based Social Security upon lingering echoes of failed Marxism. They did not understand that mixing redistribution with investment-capitalism is like mixing water and oil.

They originally sold Social Security to the public by promising that they would hold the payroll tax money in a fund earning modest interest—into something like U.S. Treasury bonds. What really happened, however, was that Congress then regularly "borrowed" the fund money to pay the general ongoing operation of the federal government. They did not in good faith put the fund money to work, as happens in capitalism, thereby earning multiples of the original deposits.

When a worker reached retirement, he was dependent on the fund increasing—more new workers depositing into the fund. He received a Social Security check from new money deducted from the payrolls of the younger, newer workers. This is redistribution. This is Ponzi at work. This system is going broke.

The solution is to take the social security and medical payroll tax money and invest it rather than redistribute it. As it is now, over half of U.S. debt is owned by China and Japan, with Russia, Germany, England, Brazil, Switzerland and others owning the rest of the debt. They get interest on that investment. Instead, put payroll tax money into a trust fund for younger workers and invest it in bonds and safe securities like U.S. Treasuries and blue chip securities. Then, don't raid the fund. Give a worker ownership in the res (means trust fund), i.e. give him ownership in the fund and its earnings.

To implement this idea, there would have to be a transition period. Perhaps some of these funds could temporarily be loaned back to a transition fund for retiring individuals to help them move from a redistribution scheme to a true capitalist investment portfolio. Plan long term; take 20 or 30 years to accomplish the transition to true public/private finance.

All the famous philanthropy trusts have investment portfolios, not redistribution schemes. Why aren't our Social Security tax receipts regarded as a trust fund to be invested in safe securities such as commodities like gold and precious metals? Why is it based on redistribution, a fallacious, atavistic idea of Karl Marx?

Finance social security the way we financed the Second World War, the atom bomb, the Hoover Dam, toll roads, the Tennessee Valley Authority, and other great public works: have the fund put trust capital to work to earn back the money necessary to pay retirees, to provide for medical security and to give them a slice of the capitalist pie.

Of course, the fund must never be administered by the government or politicians, who have a clear conflict of interest. It should be administered by independent trustees with a firewall between the fund and the government.

Actually, privately financing security for old age happens all the time. An oft-cited example was the case of several thousand employees of Galveston County, Texas who were allowed to opt out of the Social Security program in the early 1980s, and had their money placed in a private retirement plan. While employees who earned $50,000 per year would have collected $1,302 per month in Social Security benefits, the private plan was able to pay them $6,843 per month—approaching six times more. While employees who earned $20,000 per year would have collected $775 per month in Social Security benefits, the private plan paid them $2,740 per month, at the interest rates prevailing in 1996.

We find that most state pension plans invest a portion of employer and employee contributions in a mixture of stocks, bonds, real estate, etc. So it does happen all the time. The qualified fund managers invest on behalf of the employees into a general fund for the group.

Yes, what we are talking about could be regarded as a form of privatizing Social Security—more like quasi-privatizing it—but I suggest we do it gradually. Merge it into the current system. Possibly start the transition point for the switchover at middle age and lower the transition age each year.

The U.S. system of social security is based on a pyramid theory, also called a Ponzi Scheme. If this system were attempted in private enterprise, it would constitute fraud. So then why is it allowed in the public sector? When Social Security was enacted during the Roosevelt administration, the idea was to exact a tax from wages of presumably growing numbers of young workers—and *all* workers. The revenues were supposed to pay older, retiring workers when they reached the age of severely reduced productivity.

The effect, as we know, was a form of redistribution from the young to the old. Because only the old could tap the fund—there was no guarantee that any monies would be left by the time the young reached retirement age.

The misguided expectation was that in each generation, the number of young people entering the workforce would outnumber retiring people. It did not work out that way. With the population bubble of Baby Boomers now entering retirement, the increased longevity of seniors, and the fact that freeloaders and illegal immigrants are becoming ever more adept at not contributing their fair share, the system is rapidly running dry.

Let's face reality: our redistribution system is against nature and is going to go bankrupt. As we've shown, for about 75 years now, we have seen the Social Security system, this pyramid scheme, in declining operation. So why are we having such a difficult time changing something that is devoid of common sense and would otherwise constitute fraud and illegality?

Those who have difficulty with the syllogisms of logic argue that investing the fund into the marketplace would be too risky. Riskier than inevitably going broke? All those foundations—the Rockefeller's, the Vanderbilt's, the Howard Hughes', the Warren Buffet's, the Bill Gates's—didn't go broke. They were not founded on redistribution. They were not founded on a distorted idea of Robin Hood, or on the ideas of Karl Marx. So I disagree with naysayers who are against revamping the funding of Social Security or medical security. Yes, revamp it into a capitalist system.

As I have shown, without capitalism there would be no economy at all, and our present Ponzi-style Social Security system would not last even a day, let alone survive, however imperfectly, for seventy years. Without capitalism, the world would implode and the human species would perish.

Life would be so much easier if we'd just leave some room for nature to work her magic. Social Security should be based on the free market. Let nature assist with the management and operation of this complex system. Allow nature's free enterprise to simplify it.

Perhaps some thinkers who cling in their closets to Marx's arguments have not heard of the aforementioned Rockefeller Foundation, Howard Hughes Medical Institute, Kennedy Family Trusts, Bill and Melinda Gates Trusts, the Susan Thompson Buffet Charitable Trusts, or all the millions of other private Trusts that are administered by very conservative trustees and trust companies all around the world. Entire fields of law and branches of courthouses are dedicated to the administration of trusts.

In the practice of law, those fields are referred to as Wills and Trusts and are administered by the probate departments of courthouses. There are also securities—annuities, to name one—that are administered by insurance companies. By law, these securities are required to be very conservatively managed.

The additional leftist argument that in a privatized investment, inflation would not be indexed to change, is specious. Inflation generally raises some ships and sinks a good many others, but generally it raises the ship of privatized investments. Similarly, the fear that privatized Social Security would simply line the pockets of Wall Street brokers is false. Just pay brokers the way court-administered trust funds pay their trustees and managers—very conservatively, with conflicts of interest and commissions strictly banned. Fees should be paid at an hourly rate or based on the amount managed, but never on commission for that would beget a conflict of interest for the broker.

A multitude of solutions are available to correct potential abuses, including having licensed private Social Security managers or trustees act as fiduciaries after passing professional competency examinations. In response to the question of how to insulate the system from managers committing bribery, corruption, and exercising undue political influence, we could also simply incarcerate violators. Put them in jail. That will send a message.

Some countries long ago wised up and privatized their Social Security systems. Chile is one, Sweden another; even the formerly socialist-leaning United Kingdom has embraced the idea.

The Cato Institute stated: "Social Security privatization is gaining momentum worldwide. Since Chile successfully privatized its Social Security system in 1981, other countries across Latin America have begun to consider and implement similar reforms. Argentina, Colombia, El Salvador, Peru, Mexico, and Uruguay have already started privatizing their systems. With far less fanfare, Great Britain began Social Security privatization almost 20 years ago, and about three-fourths of its workers have now opted out of half the old system there."

Those who have not reversed themselves on this point, including recalcitrant, left-leaning closet Marxists in the U.S., are like the dog who loses his tail while crossing the railroad tracks: He barely, but painfully, outraces the Bolshevik train; then, when he turns to sniff the tail he lost, the Socialist train comes along and cuts off his head. In other words, don't try to resurrect what failed from a fundamental flaw the first time: it will probably kill you the second time.

In the 1990s, I had the pleasure of sitting with several Latin American presidents and dignitaries at a banquet round-table sponsored by the Institute of the Americas and the Latin American political science chair at the University of California at San Diego. My dinner companions spoke in glowing terms of the privatization of their versions of Social Security. Everyone at the table supported the concept.

Notably, each attendee at our table had received his economics education at colleges and institutes of learning, including Ivy League schools, in the U.S. These individuals seemed to have put their U.S.-gained knowledge to good use. Meanwhile within the borders of our nation, we are too mired in political logjams to think as sensibly.

Perhaps our legislative and executive branches are in the hands of liberal arts majors rather than business and economics majors. Liberal arts majors misconstrue "food for thought," believing that thought will bring food. Has anyone checked whether Socrates fed his family on thought alone? The key word is *production*.

A comment from the Heritage Foundation, a conservative think tank, as reported in Wikipedia, is noteworthy: It ". . . calculates that a 40-year-old male with an income just under $60,000, will contribute $284,360 in payroll taxes to the Social Security Trust Fund over his working life, and can expect to receive $2,208 per month in return under the current program." They claim that the same 40-year-old male, investing the same $284,360 equally weighted into treasuries and high-grade corporate bonds over his working life, would own a retirement worth $904,982, which would pay an annuity of up to $7,372 per month (assuming that the dollar volume of such investments would not dilute yields so that they are lower than averages from a period in which no such dilution occurred).

Furthermore, they argue that ". . . the 'efficiency' of the system should be measured not by costs as a percent of assets, but by returns after expenses (e.g. a 6 percent return reduced by 2 percent expenses would be preferable to a 3 percent return reduced by 1 percent expenses). Other advocates state that because privatization would increase the wealth of Social Security users, it would contribute to consumer spending, which in turn would cause economic growth."

Of course even with some sort of privatization or quasi-privatization, the greedy hands of bureaucrats and politicians must be slapped every time they try to reach into the cookie jar. They seem incapable of avoiding it.

But with privatization, the risk of creeping corruption occurring would seem far less than under our failing Ponzi system. Trillions of dollars could be very conservatively invested into the infrastructure and the economies of free world countries. Allow the fund to build up as the economy grows. Allow Social Security to pay for itself, to earn its way. Let nature's free market assist in the management of this complex system: let nature work her magic.

For those who do not earn a living and cannot contribute to the system, other reasonable means of assistance can be found. The most important aspect of implementing such a plan would be maintaining a self-executing co-opetition synthesis within it. Again, this means to let nature's free market emphasis do most of the work and drive most of the simplification. The idea is to make sure everyone, through free enterprise and business, is invested in his or her own future.

To reemphasize, this happens all the time, day in and day out, when trustees conservatively manage inheritances for their beneficiaries. It would be great incentive for the voting masses, as investors in the country's economy, to wrest for themselves the control of their financial destinies and to want their investment portfolios to do well. That way, their general motivation would be, among other things, to keep corporate taxes—all taxes, for that matter—as low as possible.

During its heyday, Rome had a safety-net social security system, but only two days' worth of each citizen's work-year was necessary to pay the taxes—versus seventy or more days in the contemporary U.S. Later, as Roman bureaucracy grew and became ever more unwieldy, Rome declined. The government became too bloated. This tells us that the best course is to slenderize government by rendering lean and efficient its insidious bureaucracies.

A good example of self-executing co-opetition is the growing practice by union pension funds of investing in business and industry. However, there is the caveat that a union must not own too great a share of its own company because, as mentioned earlier, that could become a conflict of interest.

Let's place the voting public in a position of having a built-in *beneficial* conflict of interest. You could call this a "win-win" situation. If the public wants their investment portfolios and the economy to do well, they will have to think like capitalists and seek ways to cut away the burdens of overregulation and unnecessarily and redundant high costs of government. Obviously, many details must be worked out; however, using the principle of self-executing co-opetition—synthesizing social needs (cooperation) with nature's free market (competition)—most of the problems are solvable.

Remember, this is also akin to Adam Smith's Invisible Hand. It works with little interference or manipulation by man, yet could make complex systems, such as health care, Social Security, and government education systems much simpler to guide and judiciously operate. Let nature work for you; she'll do a good job if you let her—and she's free.

A warning, though: security at the borders and ports of entry will need to be shored-up, for even more would-be immigrants will try to rush in and take advantage of the abundance and dilute the res—the bounty the people of this country created and invested in. We cannot become the world's treasure chest. Nor can we become part of a world government for that very same reason.

16

Universal Health Care, Socialized Medicine

This subject is far too complex to fully discuss in this work, but I will analyze it from the standpoint of how I would apply the scale of co-opetition.

First I will state my conclusion, and then back it up with facts and argument.

Conclusion

Restore the doctor-patient relationship. Re-energize the spirit of traditional charity; strengthen non-profit hospitals and expand competitive free-enterprise insurance coverage; lessen reliance on big government. Provide necessary and major health care through patched universal help, primarily for indigents and for those suffering catastrophic illnesses or accidents, pre-existing conditions, as well as for the approximately 40 million with little or no health insurance coverage.

Pay for the patch through true finance, not redistribution; pay through health-care savings and other innovations. The question is not *whether* to provide necessary and major health care for all. The question is *how* to provide it: (a) through redistribution and socialism? Or, (b) provide it through capitalism, utilizing the sweet spot of mother nature's magic?

Discussion

First, a 2015 update. They've discovered a 3.4 million person subsidy overpayment that will have to be paid back by the taxpayer out of refunds. Second, the employer mandate will be kicking in for firms of over 50 employees, sucking away the incentive to hire new employees. Third, reimbursements to doctors will be reduced by 43 percent. Fourth, since passage of the Act, also known as Obamacare, a very large segment of the public feels that their health care costs have increased considerably, while their quality of care has decreased. Finally, we're now burdened with the Supreme Court's decision on King v. Burwell, which otherwise could have effectively cut the guts out of the Affordable Health Care Act.

A new congress needs to go to work to correct or replace parts of the existing hastily considered law with an Act that more adequately fits with nature's asymmetric equation of balancing liberty with moral rationality. Now to the discussion:

Except for perhaps 12 percent of the population—about 40 million people—we enjoyed a relatively good health care system in the U.S. It needed fixing primarily in areas of coverage for pre-existing conditions, portability, and for those who could not afford healthcare insurance at all.

In the 1950s and 1960s, the system consisted of a pretty good mixture of "for-profit" (competition), and assistance from the government and assistance from charity (cooperation). The present administration and progressive Democrats tried to answer the health care issue by insisting on almost total government take over. They, thereby, de-emphasized help from Mother Nature (altruism, philanthropies) and the free market. I shall show that natural, free help from the market-place and traditional charity can simplify this otherwise complex system and reduce its costs. The insistence on a total government takeover makes one ponder: are echoes of Marxism subconsciously affecting our leaders? Is their recalcitrance in good faith or does it stem from a greater agenda? Won't they let the failed philosophy of Karl Marx finally expire?

They hoped that a "single payer"—generally meaning payment by the government—could purchase a rationed or reduced quantity of medical services at lower, controlled prices, thereby reducing the overall costs of providing health care. But experience in England and Canada, among other countries, shows that shortages and queues inevitably result. Further funding through redistribution becomes impractical because the population is living longer. The ratio of the older to the younger is rapidly changing, with the seniors gaining.

The economist, Dr. Milton Freidman, wisely said: "When the patient doesn't pay the bills directly and doesn't see the money leaving his pocket he is not likely to complain about the high charges. The cost then goes up." It goes up because fewer people squawk about the bill. This is the phenomenon of a "third-party payer" system (Meaning: another person pays the bill. The government could be the payer or your Elk's Lodge could be the payer).

The French health care system succeeds by avoiding such a third-party payer system. Patients pay their bills directly, but soon thereafter they receive a 70 percent reimbursement from the government or from the insurance company. But the patient sees the money flow from his wallet.

The so-called "single-payer system," on the other hand, has a different meaning. Single-payer is where the government is the only source of the payment to the doctor or health provider. No other person or entity pays the bill. Thus, in this system, the single- payer-government is in this sense *also* a so-called "third party payer." Friedman argues: get rid of "third party payer" and watch health care costs come down dramatically such as in the French system. There, medical costs per capita are about half of what we have in the U.S. The French are reputed to have the best outcome for medical care in the world.

Under the English and Canadian single-payer (government pays) systems, we've all heard of the long waiting lines. A little levity on waiting queues: in the recent Soviet Union, a farmer has finally saved enough money to buy a new car. He goes to the government distributer and is put on the list. He can pick up his car in two years. He's given the date. The customer wants to know if it's in the morning or afternoon. The official says, "Why do you care? It's two years away." The farmer replies: "Because the plumber is coming that afternoon."

In a multi-payer system (it should be called a multi-reimburser system), on the other hand (where the patient sees the money leave his wallet), not only are long queues less likely, there are often different types of cost containment offered by different health insurers. These include various sizes of deductibles or co-payments, which in turn affect the quantity of services delivered.

Over time there have been innovations in cost containment among health insurers in multi-payer systems. Out-patient surgery, which is less expensive than in-patient surgery, is now common. Pre-certification has reduced hospital admissions, and concurrent review has reduced length-of-stay in hospitals. There are a large number of health maintenance organizations (HMOs) and preferred provider organizations (PPOs), which also attempt to contain costs, as well as the traditional fee-for-service plans in the health insurance industry.

We reiterate our strong belief that the current forced-cooperation movement to universalize health care by redistribution is against nature. When Marx came up with his theories, he was not aware of the co-opetition scale. He did not synthesize (i) charity and (ii) the professional injunctions of the Hippocratic Oath (docter's ethics to protect the patient) with (iii) a measured amount of government assistance and (iv) free-market pay-for-service into an equation of co-opetition.

This brings us to the government's latest contemporary attempt. Enough sincere, pragmatic, and true competition is not part of the Affordable Health Care Act. That act seemingly is emblematic of the current disguised movement toward a redistribution-type universal health care system, a concept that appears subtly designed to lead eventually to a single-payer system (where the third-party government always pays).

It does not sufficiently draw on help from traditional, natural altruism. Sensibly nurtured and appreciated charity is not sufficiently part of The Act. Such altruism is necessary in order to foster and finance an equation for a workable health care system.

Moreover, crony-capitalism in the form of profit-making Health Management Organizations (HMOs) has crept into the traditional doctor-patient relationship. Crony-capitalism reveals itself as protectionism, offering price-fixing subsidies to the drug and pharmaceutical industry under the veil of what they call "government regulation," which take the form of conflicts of interest suffered by providers. It takes the form of an unholy alliance between drug companies and some profit-motivated providers.

The inevitable result is that the price of health care goes up for both patients and for managers of the system. And the complexity of the change has gone beyond the capacity of man to efficiently manage.

As Milton Friedman said: "Expressed as a fraction of national income, spending on medical care went from 3 percent of the national income in 1919 to 4.5 percent in 1946 to 7 percent in 1965 to a mind-boggling 17 percent in 1997 and beyond. No other country in the world approaches that level of medical spending as a fraction of national income no matter how its medical care is organized.

"The changing role of medical care in the U.S. economy is truly breathtaking. To illustrate, in 1946, seven times as much was spent on food, beverages, and tobacco than on medical care; in 1996, 50 years later, more was spent on medical care than on food, beverages, and tobacco."

Background

As of 2013, in terms of outcome—i.e. who are the healthiest—the U.S. ranks around 37th among the world's nations. France ranks first. However, the U.S. has the most state-of the- art health care facilities. Why the anomaly? "Behavioral factors, such as physical inactivity, smoking, and dietary choices, combined with [other] disparities, result in poor performance" (quoted from *International Comparisons of World Health Organization Reports*, 2000, and 2007).

A decline of U.S. ranking for outcome (but not quality) of healthcare has occurred over the last 40 years. As said, most of the decline results from lifestyle, rather than purported inadequate facilities and quality of treatment and care.

Was the U.S. health care system inadequate in the 1950s? No. It has never been inadequate when compared with the industrialized countries of the world. In fact, it has been a leader on quality, innovation, and expertize. In the past, the more prosperous nations did a better job than did the undeveloped countries in ensuring that everyone, rich or poor, or brown, black or white, or of whatever religion or ethnicity, received adequate health care.

I remember those days as a U.S. child during the Second World War and adolescent during Korea and as a young adult during the Vietnam War. For those who could afford it, health care was provided by the free market, and for those who could not, it was provided by charities, nonprofits, the Hippocratic Oath of medical professionalism—a duty imposed by virtue of medical ethics—by some local governments and the VA.

In cases of catastrophic illnesses for those suffering from severe poverty, it was provided by local, taxpayer-government-charity-supported county hospitals. Sometimes, properly, family members supplemented and assisted each other. No one went without reasonably adequate health care.

Emergency rooms handled the accidents. I don't remember hearing anyone complain about lack of availability of healthcare. Until the age of twelve, I came from a middle-class family located in a less than middle-class neighborhood. We had our share of tragedies, including deaths, severe injuries and illnesses. I confirmed my memories by reminiscing with a dear Italian immigrant lady who was poor while growing up here in the U.S. during the Depression, but is still of razor-sharp memory and mind—my 101-year-old mother, Josie.

She passed the tests and worked as an electronics technician on the B-24, among others, in aircraft war plants during the Second World War and Korea. Between wars, she continued in electronics. From blueprints, she assembled the instrument panel of Alan Shepard's space capsule while she was employed by Stromberg Carlson, San Diego. She received awards for innovation.

One of my mother's recollections is about health care in the U.S. when her family had just arrived in San Diego from Italy via Ellis Island in New York. She was nine at the time. Her father had put up all his money as a guaranty to the U.S. that the family would not go on welfare. He was proud and happy that he could afford to put up that guaranty. After discharge from Ellis Island and upon arriving in San Diego, they discovered that the local agent they had hired had bilked them out of all their guaranty money. This was 1924. Within months, my mother's younger seven year-old brother, Nicky stepped on a rusty nail and came down with tetanus. The county hospital took him in and for six months nursed him back to health. The family was not charged a dime.

Ask my mother which health system was better, that of 1924 or 2014?. She says that 1924 was, hands-down, better than this change to redistribution. She describes how people they hardly knew, good-hearted people, set up a Christmas tree in the house and flooded it with presents. She was, and still is, overwhelmed by the generosity of the people of this country. She can understand how one who never grew up in poverty can be bamboozled by propaganda.

This country was not *A Tale of Two Cities*. It was and still is by far the most generous place on earth. It did not need a radical change to redistribution. It needed tweaking of its wonderful, natural, free-market system; it already had nature's altruism as part of the equation. Natural altruism is something you will find in most people, despite misinformation to the contrary.

This doesn't mean mandated "altruism" or forced-coopera- tion. We never heard of anyone losing their home or fortune or life savings because of medical exigencies. The overwhelming character of medical care was of charity, kindness, and empathy. It wasn't a total hammock, though; you had to remain reasonably diligent in looking after the medical needs of your family and loved ones, as it should be in a co-opetitive society.

It was a very good network system, though. The nurses and other professionals and charity workers all seemed proud and happy to provide help. People were happy doing charity, happy to give extra purpose to their lives. Doctors even made house vis- its, while faith-based and other charities built and operated most of the hospitals. Philanthropists provided much of the funding, and you chose your own doctor, with the professional doctor-pa- tient relationship sometimes lasting for a lifetime.

Ambulances blared through the streets. The county hospital or the veteran's hospital provided wonderful, free medical care to the needy and destitute. Some, but not all families, bought insurance, primarily to cover catastrophic illnesses or accidents. Based on my awareness at the time, if an accident found a patient without insurance, medical bill collection generally took into consideration the ability to pay. Doctors and hospitals regularly wrote off collections rather than force patients into bankruptcy.

Was I looking through rose colored glasses? I think not. Peo- ple paid cash or with a credit card for ordinary medical needs, like you do when buying food, clothing, gas, servicing your car, or paying for vacations. If you didn't have cash, we know of the stories of doctors in rural areas taking a chicken or two instead.

Yes, there was a bit of stigma for those who had to go to a county hospital (as there was for having to collect welfare), but good medical care was provided there, and they often were places where medicine was taught.

Medicine was not a business; it was a profession. Hospitals generally were not businesses but charities. We didn't need socialized medicine in those times. I heard no complaints against the system; I was aware of no push apparent to inject radical, drastic change into the system. There is much wisdom to the phrase "If it's not broken don't fix it."

At that time we had by far the best health care in the world in terms of facilities, doctors, and services; so as a young adult I thought, why not build on what we have? Maintain it in good condition, update it, and cherish it. Polish it. Tweak it. When what you have works well, enhance and improve but don't abolish, destroy, and start all over. If you radically try to fix or change something with unknown dimensions of complexity, you run the risk of unforeseen consequences.

ONE SIZE SHOE DOES NOT FIT ALL;
WE ARE NOT EUROPE

So what do we learn from that? We already know that one shoe doesn't fit all feet; the people of impoverished nations may need some form of socialized medicine. European nations experienced greater impact from the world wars than had we in the U.S. Perhaps deficiencies in hospital care, doctors and ambulances existed there. But since serious deficiencies did not then exist here in the U.S., there was no rush to take over one-sixth of the economy in order to install nationalized health care.

Why do that when all that was needed was a patch for indigents and the uninsured? For the vast majority, routine health matters—such as check-ups, annual exams, and the like—could be paid for like buying groceries or fuel at the gas station or paying for a weekend vacation.

Why is that not also true today? Why not just patch-in help for the maybe 40 million people we presume are not adequately medically protected? Why force the vast majority of the public, the remaining 270 million people who are generally happy with their medical coverage and who like and want to keep their doctors, into a massive, super-complex, forced-cooperation, government-controlled system intended to solve the needs of 12 percent of the population, especially since it doesn't seem to solve the problems of that 12 percent; it appears to compound them.

You will say, that's probably because we need to get enough money to finance those 40 million uninsured people. So do we take the money from those who can afford it and give it to those who can't? That is the cardinal question. No. We can use Mother Nature to work her magic, simplifying and reducing costs. We've already answered that, and evolved to see the immorality of one tribe raiding another. We learned that we can trade with each other instead; that we evolved to discover capitalism, the free market, the win-win miracle of nature.

We can bring together a combination of the free market, charity, and government in a symphony of moving parts to perfect and accomplish our objective. There are multipayer systems in other parts of the world, at near half the cost as America's. Those systems are not "socialized" medicine, yet they appear to be working fine. We've spoken of the French system for example; the French strongly feel their system is not socialized medicine, it is multi-payer—meaning payments can come from the patient, private insurers, government or charity. It's based on re-imbursement to the patient. The patient actually takes the money out of his wallet, pays, and then gets 70 percent reimbursement. As we said, a French person sees the money flow from his pocket as he pays; Thus, the patient's natural tendency is not to wastefully spend the money—to not be a hypochondriac or rush to the expensive ER for a hangnail.

So what is socialized medicine for us in the U.S.? The very conservative would say it's the crown jewel propaganda tool of anachronistic Marxism. It is the shoe horn for imposing forced-cooperation on us all. It is the slow-cooker spa that seems warm and pleasant before it lulls you to sleep and kills you. A conservative would say that the theory does not reward hard work and production. If you get the same lifestyle whether you work hard or hardly work, why work?

Let's look at it from the viewpoint of our co-opetition synthesis scale. Recall that our system of health care became naturally modernized between the 1930s and the 1980s by people insuring against the risk of catastrophic accident or illness. Innovative insurance companies and agents sold those packages the same way they sold automobile insurance or fire insurance for the farm. The packages were promoted by private enterprise. On a national level the government tended not to get involved.

However, in Europe—primarily England, whether because of greater impact from the war or from an unfavorable entrepreneurial climate brought on by persistent socialist voices—the insurance systems apparently did not fulfill peoples' needs for healthcare at the level enjoyed in the U.S. As a result, European governments stepped in with universal health care. By forcing cooperation through regulation and taxation, the governments redistributed the income and assets of the people and allotted to each and everyone a portion for health care needs.

There is no denying that this idea came straight from Karl Marx and his followers. Bolstering what I've said, Nobel Prize-winning economist Milton Friedman in his book, *Capitalism and Freedom: Fortieth Anniversary Edition,* said that nobody spends somebody else's money as wisely or as frugally as he spends his own. Direct payments made by a third party, e.g. by government or insurance companies are the reason in the U.S. we spend much more money per capita on health care than in any other country on earth, and the people of the U.S. have less to show for it.

OUR ORIGINAL SELF-OPERATING, FREE-MARKET INSURANCE SYSTEM TAPPED THE FORCES OF NATURE FOR SUCCESS

During the early 1900s, our more natural healthcare system seemed to be working, at least well enough to stave off the mounting wave of socialism from Europe. I vividly remember joining a law firm in the 1970s that, in order to attract good employees and young lawyers, provided health insurance plans at our expense. No one forced us to do so. Competition in the work force, together with intuitive altruism, nudged us in that direction.

Moreover, all the young lawyers in the firm were expected to do *pro bona* legal work for indigents for at least one month of each year. The firm subsidized us, and I walked my share of acquitted defendants out of criminal court(public defenders were not yet in operation in our city).

Thus, there was less pressure here in the U.S. to install socialized medicine than was the case in parts of Europe. Perhaps the attitudes of people of Europe were not as generous as were the attitudes of the public in the U.S; I really don't know. Except for a limited group of countries, Europeans essentially left free-market competition out of their reasoning—nobody at the time was aware of a co-opetition formula.

Government forced-cooperation, in the form of redistribution monopolized thinking. Thus, they left no room for the workings of nature to simplify the growing complexity of managing their government-controlled medical systems.

We know that competition between the elements of the free market naturally forces a strong element of efficiency into any system. Europe relied primarily on government management to ration and force this hoped-for efficiency, but "government efficiency" is a bit of an oxymoron. Perhaps Europe was too far down the path of socialism to reflect on that.

Here, years later, the fact that the Affordable Health Care Act was 2,600 pages with multitudes of additional thousands of pages to codify and regulate seems *prima facie* that the subject is too complex for man to effectively manage.

THEN, IN THE 1970s AND 1980s, THE EXTREMES AT EACH END OF THE CO-OPETITION SCALE FOULED-UP MEDICAL CARE

Starting in the 1960s and 1970s, supposedly to improve efficiency, control costs, and avoid the prospect of socialized medicine, alternatives were tried. The competitive side—the free-enterprise side—offered the alternative of having private, for-profit *management organizations* force more efficiency into health care. This 1973 idea shows an innate blindness to the prospect of allowing nature's intuitive magic to provide the desired efficiency. Not only is it idiocy to hope that government will inject efficiency, it's also idiocy to think that private *for-profit* organizations will reduce costs to the patient. It's idiocy because the costs businesses save in squeezing out more efficiency they take back in profits. This results in a wash at best, or at worst, it results in much higher healthcare costs.

Neither solution calls out to nature's intuitive altruism to accomplish efficiency.

So how did this profit-based middleman come into being? It was the creation of a Democratic Congress under the leadership of Senator Ted Kennedy and Republican President Richard Nixon. They passed and signed into law the Health Management Organization Act of 1973. Among other things, the Act mandated that all companies employing more than 25 people must have an HMO manage the details of cost, coverage, and types of treatment.

This gave even greater control to insurance companies, which adopted the role of overseer of the claims and benefits they paid and what kinds of treatment were appropriate. Is that not a conflict of interest waiting to happen? The doctor and the patient should decide this, not a third-party overseer. The insurance company didn't go to medical school and become certified to advise on whether a biopsy test should be given.

The HMOs or Health Management Organizations, thus, introduced a for-profit middleman into the system—between doctors and their patients. Gone, or watered down, was traditional charity and the ethical medical duty embraced within the Hippocratic Oath. Now it was all business.

Does that sound like the injection of maybe too much competition? Not surprisingly, such a change in the system began to displace the cooperative instincts of charity and altruism that had composed the "liberal," side of the health-care scale.

What have been the consequences of the HMO Act of '73? The cost of health care is now out of sight. Does a correlation there exist? The original reason for the HMO was to reduce costs. Now the middleman takes a cut of profit, which adds to the overall cost of health care—make any sense to you? I didn't think so.

234 / A Primal Wisdom

The Affordable Health Care Act places another giant cook into the allegorical kitchen, spoiling the soup even more. Don't the failures of the rollout of AHCA demonstrate that universal healthcare is too complex for total government management to handle? The president had to exempt and defer for a year big labor, big business, and then even Congress from the Act's mandates. If the Act was not perfected enough at that time for big business, big labor, and Congress, then why was it "perfected" enough for the nation's vulnerable middle class and seniors?

Don't forget why socialism finally collapsed in the Soviet Union: Marx's idea of totally managing economies was flawed. It's too complex for man to handle without the help of mother nature, and it was funded based on the ideology of redistribution rather than by true finance. Personal dependence on government burgeoned and personal independence fell flat.

We need to come up with a healthcare plan that reaches an ultimate synthesis of the free market and charity and some government—but the synthesis must come from true finance, not redistribution. We repeat: redistribution is a giant Ponzi scheme. It robs Peter to pay Paul.

Senator John McCain's idea of more competition between the insurance carriers is a good start. He wants tax credits to go to people so they can pick their own insurance companies, doctors and healthcare providers. Risk pools could be set up at the state level to buy insurance for those who are unemployed or who have pre-existing conditions. Allow insurance companies to compete across state lines. The Feds could subsidize where needed.

Congressman Tom Price of Georgia suggested a similar tax credit idea. Dr. Ben Carson suggests health savings accounts, either through tax credits or funded by government from payroll taxes. But don't raise taxes or increase the size of government; increase the portability of health care coverage for those changing or losing jobs, along with insuring for pre-existing conditions. Allow pharmaceutical companies to compete worldwide if the product qualifies with the FDA.

The idea is that true competition between participants lowers costs and simplifies the whole system. On the cooperation side of this proposed health care solution, let a combination of philanthropists, service clubs, nonprofits, charities, moral/professional duties imposed by the Hippocratic Oath, and government do their thing and synthesize their efforts as they see fit.

In a recent interview with Bill Gates, Neil Cavuto asked, somewhat facetiously, why Gates didn't give foundation money direct to the Haitian government to administer rather than give it directly to earthquake victims. The answer of course was that private foundations and charities are far more efficient and less wasteful than are governments.

To give an extreme example of waste, why should society pay to treat a hypochondriac's hangnail? Non-catastrophic health care for run-of-the-mill needs should not be provided for free, except to the truly indigent and worthy. For them, the first line of defense should be provided, as in the past, by philanthropies and charity, together with, as the last resort, some help from government.

Yes, rely on the altruistic callings of mother nature. For example, in the late '90s, five hundred million dollars provided by Rotary to the World Health Organization practically wiped out polio worldwide. Only as a last resort and to fill in between the cracks should the federal government become a part of the healthcare equation.

Presumably, the rest of the people—the moderately well-to-do middle class—are able to pay cash or credit for mundane, ordinary healthcare needs, or pay premiums for insurance for their major healthcare requirements. Many would probably opt for catastrophic insurance only.

Yes, the rich would be able to afford better health care. But we already have minimum standards set by medical schools, medical boards, professional insurance agencies, hospitals, juries, judges and the like. Keep all that in place, of course.

On the conservative side of the equation, wouldn't it make sense to stop subsidizing crony-capitalism? Subsidies interfere with the free market; they interfere with the workings of nature. Why subsidize an HMO? Why subsidize any insurance company, for that matter, except maybe for financial help on pre-existing conditions. But even then you'd have to study the proposed subsidy very carefully.

Let competition fight such practices as built-in obsolescence and the sky-high costs of FDA approval, which keeps the little innovator-guy from competing with the giants. The cost of *patent* maintenance and approval should also be looked at to make sure competition from the little guy isn't stifled. If he can't afford to keep paying his required patent maintenance costs he could lose his patent.

On the issue of mandating everyone to have health insurance, all is not what first meets the eye. The reason for mandating is to pool the risk, spread costs, lower premiums, and subsidize those who have preexisting conditions. Supporters say it's like requiring all car drivers to carry insurance. What's wrong with that?

What's wrong is that it's not at all like driver's insurance. Driver's insurance is mandated to protect victims of accidents. It's mandated liability insurance, not protection for injuries for the negligent party. Driving is a privilege, not a right. The state doesn't want anyone on the road who can't pay for injuring someone else. To a limited extent, auto insurance companies pool the risk of good drivers with bad drivers in order to provide lower cost insurance to all. To that very limited extent, the cost of premiums for bad drivers is, thereby, partially subsidized. However for the most part, insurance companies generally penalize the bad or accident prone drivers; they increase the premiums or deductibles the year after they suffer an accident or get a few speeding tickets. The practice also serves the good purpose of teaching the bad drivers a lesson. Note how bad drivers tend to become a lot more careful when they see that their bad habits cost them money. Thus, there is no substantial redistribution of "wealth" from good drivers to bad.

Health care insurance, on the other hand, is a far different proposition. Your health is your prerogative, not a privilege. It is you (and your family) you want to protect, not some third party. The AHCA mandates for health insurance, results in charging younger, healthier persons greater than their proportionate cost for medical care, and using the excess funds to subsidize the risk for insuring older persons and those with preexisting conditions.

We're back to the redistribution of wealth, which is a taking without fair compensation and denies equal protection of the law—two violations of the Constitution. In other words, the law discriminates. It discriminates against the young and healthy.

But by a single vote in 2012, the Supreme Court declared that the mandate is actually a tax, which means it doesn't violate the Constitution. Okay, I get that. But isn't the *effect* still, in substance, a violation of equal protection as a form of discrimination? Isn't it an unlawful taking? In law school, we'd argue the maxim: substance over form.

In 1913, the country ratified the constitutional amendment

that allowed for progressive income taxing—discriminatory taxing against higher-earners. Does that solve its clash with the 14th
Amendment anti-discrimination issue? In 2010, the administration sold the health insurance mandate to Congress by vehe-
mently denying that it was a tax, but this was a bait and switch
tactic. Later before the Supreme Court, the administration
reversed itself in order to avoid "violating-the-constitution argument" and sold the mandate to the Court as a tax.

Wasn't this also a bait and switch on the American people? Is
it proper to misrepresent to the public the meaning and effect of
a law if such representation accomplishes the objective of getting
the law passed. Do the ends justify the means?

If in fact intent to deceive was there, isn't such an Orwellian
tactic? Would it have Machiavelli written all over it? I will let others judge this one. Nevertheless, we live under a democracy, still;
we the people must base our decisions on truths, not apparent
misinformation.

A driver can choose not to drive, to take a train, or taxi instead.
But under the Affordable Health Care Act all adults must have
health insurance or pay a fine, and if they fail to pay the fine they
might even wind up in jail. It's like a military draft administered
not by a draft board but by the tax collectors.

Were apparent inefficiencies of the AHCA the reasons the
government exempted big business, big labor, and various government employees from the first year of the mandate? The
people without lobbyists—the vulnerable, individuals, and small
entrepreneurs—were left taking the brunt for the others. As
Jay Leno said, "Before they went on vacation, Congress voted
to exempt them from Obamacare. They gave themselves a special exemption because they thought it was too expensive. So the
people who voted for Obamacare for us voted to exempt them-

selves from it. You know how doctors take the Hippocratic Oath? Congress apparently takes the 'Hypocritic Oath.'"

The act of exempting themselves is very probably a violation of the equal protection clause of the Constitution. In other words, the exemption discriminates against the individual plan holders. Was the motivation in giving those problematic promises in selling the Act excused by the mantra "the ends justify the means?" Again if so, isn't this is tactic unfitting of democracy?

Why didn't the conservatives come up with their own plan? They did. Over a period of more than ten years, a multitude of proposals and plans dealing with the critical issues of healthcare had been proposed by everyone from President George W Bush to Governor Romney to John McCain, Dr. Ben Carson, Congressman Price and many others. They advocated that the whole system did not need fixing, only a patch was necessary for the approximately 12 percent with pre-existing conditions, portability issues and indigence—a fix the Republicans for years had tried to get the Senate and the Administration to talk about (see "Seriously? The Republicans Have No Health Plan?" *Forbes*, Chris Conover, 8-28-2013).

The administration said, "we won!" so they refused to negotiate at all. I'd hoped they would at least negotiate the common sense incorporation of a synthesis of government, free-market and charity into a simpler, mother-nature-assisted, less costly system—a system with the markings of what we had 60 years ago.

How to Fix It

But it seems now that the real unspoken issue was not merely whether *to* fix the system, but it was *how* to fix it—(i) with an ideologically driven socialistic plan, or (ii) fix it with a free-market, mother nature assisted plan?

THE SOLUTION

The solution to healthcare reform is to get back to the synthesis of competition and cooperation. Let nature do her magic. On the competitive side, foster laws and programs that maximize competition between insurance companies, hospitals, doctors, providers, and pharmaceutical companies—companies that cross state and international lines. Carefully monitor and prosecute price fixers. And don't forget to let the patient compete by having "skin in the game" so he will be inclined to voice concern over what he is charged; he can go elsewhere if he believes he was charged too much.

On the cooperation side, foster laws and programs that restore advantages to nonprofit medical providers and hospitals, as in the past. And let Mother Nature have her way, her effect, with the for-profits. The goal is to have more competition between the for-profit middlemen, such as for the for-profit HMOs. Let the free market be the governing loop to trim their profits back to reasonable size, if too high. Or maybe they'll seek easier ways to make a dollar outside this part of the medical field.

There should be little room for their *for profit* slice of the medical care pie if they don't really contribute a benefit to the system. Remember, the for-profit HMO novo-middleman was generally not around before 1973. Remember the analogy to Diamond's prehistoric tribe: a member who doesn't earn his keep would have probably found himself ostracized or homeless.

Furthermore, encourage philanthropies and charities with limited government support to provide for part of the needs of the indigent. High co-pays and deductibles will keep down frivolous visits to providers. Have independent review boards with no conflicts of interest judge whether a provider is charging too much, or providing unnecessary or excessive medical services.

And make sure enough doctors, nurses, and medical techs are coming into the practice. Reduce the flood on emergency rooms. One serious cause is illegal immigration. Secure our borders, thereby reducing the ER cost of medical care.

The Republican plan has a lot of things right, but it has to shake off some crony-capitalism which I believe could have been negotiated away but for the Administration's political recalcitrance about refusing even to negotiate. The Republicans speak of tort reform, purchasing insurance across state lines, expanding health savings accounts, ensuring access for patients with pre-existing conditions, and permanently prohibiting taxpayer funding of abortion. They have argued these points for ten years or more. Their arguments fell on the deaf ears of the liberal left, a Democratic Congress or two, and a few ideologically-driven presidents.

"Fell on deaf ears:" Why? I believe the deafness was driven by an echo of a subconscious, brainwashed Marxist ideology favoring redistribution; and for the conscious ones, healthcare was the way for them to get the ideological wedge into the door. The true motivation factor of the intransigence of the Democrats, many believe, is that a deal with conservatives would mean they would lose their chance to force their veiled ideology, their chance to force redistribution.

On the other hand, I would apply a co-opetitive asymmetric balance to the conservative plan. I would eliminate their tort reform requirement and severely modify their stand against abortion. I'll explain why, but first, here are the good things about the plan.

On crossing state lines to buy insurance: the Republicans would eliminate the crony-capitalism of insurance companies in the states that don't want extra competition. On expanding health savings accounts: Health Savings Accounts (HSAs) are popular as they provide cost-effective health insurance to those who might otherwise go uninsured.

The Republicans would improve HSAs by making it easier for patients with high-deductible health plans to use them to obtain access to quality care. They would repeal and replace the Affordable Health Care Act, which prevents the use of these savings accounts to purchase over-the-counter medicine.

On ensuring that those with pre-existing conditions can get insurance: the Republicans would expand state high-risk pools, reinsurance programs (states' insuring the insurance companies to help them pay the claims of those with, for example, pre-existing conditions) and reduce the cost of coverage. They would make it illegal for an insurance company to deny coverage to anyone on the basis of a pre-existing condition, eliminate annual and lifetime spending caps, and prevent insurers from dropping a person's coverage just because the person gets sick. They would incentivize states to develop innovative programs that lower premiums and reduce the number of uninsured Americans.

Why do some parts of the Republican plan not result in a co-opetitive, asymmetric balance:

First, there is the issue of eliminating all taxpayer funding for abortion, including abortion subsidies to insurance companies, and of giving conscientious protections for health care providers—the doctors, nurses, pharmacies, and hospitals that refuse to provide abortions or for the day-after pills.

Instead, why not eliminate the funding only for taxpayers who consider abortion against their religious or moral precepts? Simply put a box to check on the tax returns of those who do not wish to fund abortion. They thereby exercise their individual, competitive position.

Earmark those funds that would otherwise go for abortions, for apportionment among the other federal programs; apportion on a *pro rata* basis—in the same proportions as all the other taxpayers. If there's an issue with earmarking taxes as I suggest, let the tax experts find the way so that people morally or religiously opposed to abortion in all cases are not forced to indirectly pay for them.

My 101-year old mother used to say, "Where there is a will there is a [proper] way." For those who approve of their taxes going to abortions, Congress can haggle out under what conditions it would fund them; e.g., not for late term pregnancies.

Tort Reform:

is socialism at work. Here, conservatives favoring tort reform have become unwitting pawns of medical-malpractice insurance companies, and have fallen afoul of their anti-socialist principles. (Note: I am not a so-called "trial lawyer." I specialized mainly in business, corporate, maritime and real estate law.)

Insurers keep harping about "tort reform," but when you think about it, isn't tort reform just a subsidy to malpractice insurance companies? Government-forced nullification of free market jury awards is a form of über-cooperation. The free market—as when the juries award their damages—is when nature does her work. Furthermore, in practice, it's a very rare occurrence indeed where damages *actually paid* are excessive.

The courts themselves have the power to reverse over-the top damage awards, and regularly do so. They also have the power to throw out frivolous lawsuits up front, and exact penalties against plaintiffs and sometimes their attorneys for having brought a specious action; and they often do this. Little known is the fact that attorneys are officers of the court. They ethically may not deceive the court or jury. Moreover, the courts have motivation to reduce the load on their calendars. That system needs neither help nor advantage from government in the form of tort reform.

The practice—on the competition side of the coopetition scale—of filing lawsuits against the rare incompetent medical practitioner/provider, and hospitals, or from lawsuits in the field of products liability is a good thing. It reduces the need for a consumer protection bureaucracy and the accompanying expense needed to enforce its regulations. Lawsuits reduce consumer dependency on the government, which is otherwise becoming necessary in order to nursemaid those dependents through life.

There is no denying that the consumer has at least some responsibility to be aware of charlatans, quacks, and swindlers. The maxim of Caveat Emptor is still alive. Along with the defense from lawyers on the insurance side, threat of litigation is still nature's last backstop for resolving issues.

I dislike being personal about this, but I definitely have a bias. Full disclosure: I lost both my father and my married daughter in separate incidents of serious medical and hospital malpractice. This, despite diligent, best efforts on the family's part to avoid such calamities.

In my daughter's case, the HMO assigned a nurse-practitioner to do the exam. She misdiagnosed. She said, "Nothing to worry about." The HMO was avoiding the cost of a real doctor and the cost of a routine skin biopsy. Six months later it was too late.

In my father's case, a hospital nurse tightened restraints to prevent an alert, ambulatory elderly patient from getting out of bed—provided no auxiliary oxygen, thereby unwittingly cutting off breathing. Ask most families; they'll tell you their own stories.

Remember the reasons for punitive damage awards: generally it is to punish the wrongdoer for intentially commiting the bad act. In the Ford Pinto case of Grimshaw v Ford Motor Co. of the middle 1970s, the jury found that the manufacturer kept making and selling cars with defective gas tanks even though it was aware that the tanks were causing horrendous rear-end collision explosions. It was cheaper to pay occasional wrongful death damages than to correct the gas tanks. The 122 million-dollar punitive damage award in free market litigation solved that problem. The court-reduced damages, later confirmed by the appellate court, finally amounted to only several millions dollars.

The same court reduction result was true of the tobacco cases, where it was alleged that the manufacturer had manipulated nicotine levels, making smokers even more susceptible to nicotine addiction. A court reduced awared was similarly true of the McDonald's coffee case. According to the reports, where boiling coffee fell on a woman's lap and groin, causing third-degree burns over six percent of her body; the burns severely scarred her, requiring skin grafting. The evidence showed that over 700 prior scalding complaints had been made to the defendant, yet it kept heating its coffee to 170 degrees.

Most other places that sell coffee, allegedly, kept the temperature somewhat below that. On its own, the court cut the 2.3 million award down to $680,000—including compensatory damages of $200,000 plus punitive damages of $480,000. The parties, thereafter, settled for a confidential amount.

The system handled it; the free market handled it without the interference of big-government. So-called "tort reform"—as previously said, is a euphemism for insurance company crony-capitalism. If the Republicans would eliminate tort-reform from their suggested health plans for America, don't you think a huge percentage of the so-called trial lawyers would find no further need to lobby against the ill-conceived idea of tort reform? Instead, they would more freely support a conservative approach to political science. The idea of tort reform is advocacy for more regulation and bigger government—yet big government is something conservatives profess to oppose!

Speaking of limiting damages through so-called tort reform, many years ago, I had a case involving the air crash of a DC-3 in Mexico that killed several Americans. The amount of damages allowable in the Mexican version of tort reform is very low— paltry you could say. Important to the damage claim was the question of where did the trip begin, in San Diego, or Tijuana, Mexico? "Tort reform" damages in Mexico being equivalent to four cans of beans (A relic of the effects of Mexican-style "socialism.") it was necessary to prove U.S. jurisdiction for the claim. If the trip began in the U.S., reasonable damages were awardable at that time under California law.

We proved that the trip began in the U.S. and thus were able to satisfactorily settle the case. The people killed, all employees of Caterpillar Corporation, were being flown to the salt-works at the Black Warrior Lagoon in Baja, Mexico. The Mexican company provided a van ride from San Diego to Tijuana, from where the plane took off for the lagoon. A Mexican company reputedly owned the salt-works and either owned or chartered the DC-3.

Insurance companies, doctors, and hospitals argue that the cost of litigation is too expensive and causes the cost of health care to rise too high. If the insurance carriers really want to avoid litigation, these groups should, in good faith, pay legitimate claims up front and refrain from using the pressure tactic of trying to drag the last dollar out of oft-times hapless claimants. Plaintiff's lawyers often have to fund the litigation themselves and can find themselves hundreds of thousands and even millions of dollars in debt before they get a settlement. In the opinion of many, the failure of the insurance company to quickly pay a legitimate claim is oft times in bad faith.

So, here is my suggestion. Generally, the professional insurance carrier insures only the doctor or the health care provider, not the third-party patient-clamant. If the carriers would agree to be subject to "bad faith" damages if they do not in good faith promptly pay a legitimate claim of the third-party patient, I could then go along with some so-called tort reform.

We lawyers know that potential extraordinary damages for bad faith denial of a claim, otherwise not generally available with third-party claims, might induce the carrier to promptly settle legitimate claims.

The lawyers on both sides know the true story on this one. Ask any one of them. Look at the true statistics.

THE MOUSE THAT ROARED SYNDROME; THE U.S. INDIRECTLY SUBSIDIZED EUROPEAN HEALTH CARE

A further thought on European-style socialized medicine and the reality that one shoe does not fit all:. *The Mouse that Roared,* the hilarious 1959 film starring Peter Sellers, depicted a tiny fictional kingdom in the Alps that started a one-day war with the U.S. The kingdom surrendered immediately. They wanted to get serious U.S. foreign aid money, which historically was, and is still, U.S. policy—a policy of paying for "hoped-for-alliances."

The U.S still continues to supply massive military protection for many European, Middle Eastern, and Asian countries—with over 700 bases and 380,000 troops on foreign soil. (Global Research.com, 2015)) Where do you think those troops spend most of their paychecks?

The foreign aid burden to the U.S. in 2013 was $50.6 billion (Wikipedia), but on top of that, America paid trillions of dollars over the years for stationing troops and bases on foreign soil. Since WWII, that policy has saved those countries tremendous Military Expense; the U.S. paid for, and provided them much of their military protection. America had over a million troops on foreign soil in 1968—mostly engaged in training foreign soldiers.

Had those countries been forced to pay for their own military protection during the last 50 years, they may have been hard pressed to afford their European–style socialized medicine. In this indirect way, hasn't America massively subsidized—perhaps unwittingly—all sorts of government-funded ventures of these countries, including their versions of universal health care?

There is a strong argument that, in this way, the U.S. paid for the crutches that enabled foreign government dependency to spread. No wonder foreign workers can take long vacations, and they can say we Americans work too hard. At least Rome got some reimbursement through taxation of their far off lands. As one current example, where would South Korea stand with its government entitlement and health programs if she had to pay for all her own military protection? I ask the same question of all the other countries within America's protective shield.

17

Summary

Let us refresh what we've said in this book: As I define the terms, "cooperative" conduct includes within it such diverse sub-behaviors as giving, unifying, bonding, collectivism, forced or über-cooperation, totalitarianism, socialism, and big government, among many others including even gravity and order.

On the other hand, "competitive" conduct encompasses such diverse sub-behaviors as taking, separating, individualism, freedom, and liberty, among many others. It includes the dispersal of energy, repelling particles, entropy, and chaos.

One example of the synthesis of cooperative and competitive conduct is capitalism, i.e. free enterprise. In the recipe for a thriving economy, we find the strong cooperative elements of trade, ethics, trust and confidence, and the adherence to business law and business treaties. But such cooperative conduct is fused with the competitive drive for achieving the highest and best price, increasing profits, and keeping the business enterprise going.

Growth is a big part of sustaining any thriving economy for most systems. Thus, asymmetric weight on the side of competition must usually exist in order to fertilize growth. To illustrate this principle we used the metaphor of the outrigger canoe. (See the cover of this book.) Piled into the main hull are all the competitive, free-enterprise elements of the synthesis, but fixed out at the end of the spars is the pontoon, i.e., the outrigger itself. In it are housed ethics, business law, and regulation.

The outrigged pontoon is loaded with just enough weight to keep the canoe from capsizing in a storm, but not so much as to slow the canoe down. The fulcrum of balance between the pontoon and the canoe is located in the spars, very close to the main hull. That asymmetric balance, with emphasis on competition and growth, is how a good economy should work.

We find that this fusion of cooperation and competition exists in all of nature, in all conceivable forms. If we allow it to work for us it will simplify all systems, including the very complex.

One example that comes to mind is how Communism failed every time it was tried. Why? Because total management of an economy is too complex and fraught with unforeseen consequences for man to decipher. It is like a giant hanging mobile: touch one piece and be surprised at what other piece across its expanse moves.

Also, the Marxist idea of trying to finance old age benefits and universal healthcare by redistribution of money is not "financing" at all. Rather, it is a form of raiding, something ancient competing tribes commonly did to each other before they became civilized enough to become better at trading. "Redistribution" is just a euphemism for theft or forced labor. It can never be just.

We've evolved and learned that the true fulcrum point for achievement of good and meaningful social and medical security benefits is a combination of the free market, capitalism, philanthropy and some government—the equation of co-opetition.

I believe that, in general, cultural values and controls should be preserved and nurtured; however, some less-desirable cultural traditions have rightfully been outstripped by our speedy rise to modernism. For example, who would choose to reinstitute the ancient custom of parents contracting their barely grown daughters into marriage? Dispense with that, but restore the family and the values it engendered. That alone will solve immeasurable social problems.

The best approach is to substitute logic—human intelligence and wisdom—whenever the abandonment of cultural controls threatens the *ultimate synthesis.*

In this light, we can see that the process of finding answers to the great questions and problems that affect us and our world is akin to achieving the proper synthesis—the ultimate synthesis—between order (cooperation) and chaos (competition). This is accomplished by synthesizing the dual drives of competition and cooperation to find the sweet spot between them..

Most ways of finding this point of synthesis come from nature's intuitive unification of cooperation and competition. Unquestionably with the use of our minds, we have the capability to destroy this world, but that would be contrary to our basic nature.

Yes, we might be on a course of destroying our host, the earth, but not because we *intend* to do so. The greatest likelihood, and that which is most consistent with our basic nature, is that we will use our gifts of intelligence and wisdom to partner with nature and, when necessary, delicately guide this world into a symphony of life. That is what we are programmed to accomplish. One of our strongest drives is to enable our genes to replicate and pro-create. That won't happen if we destroy the earth.

By wisely directing the internal logic of our minds with the touch of a co-opetitive hand weighted, usually, on the side of competition, we can defeat the factors—the distortions of nature—that might otherwise destroy our quest for synthesis. It is our *minds*, then, rather than a plague or HIV or the bomb or totalitarianism or mob rule that become Gregory Bateson's "governing loop."

Our minds are the sentries that will keep Adam Smith's Invisible Hand free and working. Our minds are part of the equation for self-executing co-opetition—finding the sweet spot between order and chaos—finding the ultimate synthesis. We were born with it. The universe was born with it. Truly, this force resonates from nature. It is our primal wisdom.

Acknowledgments

I am indebted to every one of those who helped evidence the universality of co-opetition: my publisher, Bettie Youngs of Bettie Youngs Book Publishers, who inspired bringing this book to print and who graciously put up with my changes. Thanks to her group: Adrian Pitariu for the overall cover design; senior editor Mark Clements who masterfully edited the text content; Jane Hagaman who not only designed my previous books *Universal Co-opetition*, and *The Tortoise Shell Game*, a novel, but has worked her magic on this book as well; and, to Jazmin Gomez for proofreading all three. Many thanks also to computer artist Ted Packman for the contribution of his work *Bestlines*, from which we took the cover background—depicting a synthesis of order and chaos, and to Chico Koch Alarco who superimposed the outrigger canoe—symbolically depicting a well-operating economy.

A heartfelt thanks, as well, to all those who contributed in some way to bring this work to life: recently departed retired Scripps oceanographer Meredith "Rip" Sessions, Starbucks pals— philosophic dialectics psychologists, Fred Marasco and Andrew

Paslawski and author David Bowles, Ph.D.—for our discussions on co-opetition; my college political science professor Dr. Henry L. Janssen, SDSU; my friend, former Ambassador to Argentina, Ted Gildred for inviting me to the Institute of the Americas banquettes and introducing Latin American dignitaries; bestselling author Spencer Johnson, M.D. who urged me to write books on the syntheses of competition and cooperation. Special thanks goes to Barbara Mansfield Asaro, with her strong and patient listening ear, who is the mother of our children, Dean, Stephanie, Valarie, and in memory of our daughter Audrey, to whom I also dedicate this latest book.

I thank likewise the graduate students who, in the 1980s, helped research and confirm the application of my theories for various academic disciplines. Their names were lost in a move. I would appreciate hearing from them should they come across this published work. And special thanks to Point Loma High school buddy Ronald D. Smith, Ph.D. USC, who later at Arizona State University, was probably the most popular history professor who ever lived, and co-author of *Against the Grain,* for reviewing my early draft and for his spellbinding historical camp-fire yarns while on Lake Powell adventures with our kids and families.

All my opinions, statements and theories given or made in this book are strictly my own, and those named above should not be regarded as having approved, adopted, or disapproved of them.

Appendix

Notes on realms within realms, or triangulation, from anthropological inquiry at end of Chapter 3:

Generally this situation is applied in a two-step process. An example would be two or more suitors competing for the same girl (we sometimes refer to that as the "love triangle"). Other examples could be two or more people competing for the same job, award, or resource; or—two or more countries competing for the future site of the Olympic Games.

In such circumstances, we would start our co-opetitive analysis by examining the cooperative and competitive tension between the competitors, and find the synthesis position—the point of unification of cooperating and competing—between them; that is, between two sides of the triangle.

We would then analyze the cooperative/competitive tension between the competitors and the goal; for example, between the boys on two sides of the triangle and the girl on the remaining side.

In other words, we would first analyze two sides of a triangle and place the synthesis position between the competitors. Then we would analyze the third side, between the competitor(s) and the goal.

When discussing this issue in parts of this work, I also referred to "realms within realms." In that context, "realms" could correlate to "triangulation." The animals in the inner realm of a pond in the forest may be affected by the movement of planets in the outer realm of the solar system—as in climate change. For example, the animals may begin cooperating in a symbiotic relationship in order to survive, that is, to "compete" with the conditions resulting from change due to movement of the planets. More than two entities or elements may be involved, hence "triangulation."

Unbalanced Universe,
continuation from the end of Chapter 4:

On further notes on physics: it could be argued, though the conclusion is not necessary to my theory, that contrary to the dreams of theoretical physicists, one "grand unification force" controlling all matter and energy might not exist after all. Instead, two countervailing forces of cooperation (order) and competition (chaos) working together in a dynamic synthesis may prove to exist.

But I propose another possibility you probably haven't heard before: the universe seeks to return to a normal state of quiescence. By quiescence, I mean a state in which virtual particle pairs of matter and antimatter fill the universe. Under this theory, both matter and anti-matter represent a symmetry of virtual matter, but with opposite charges. Thus, the virtual particles con-

tinuously annihilate one another, and a state of nothingness persists until something triggers a big bang.

The trigger could be a random event of turbulence or distortion produced by gravity or a spooky convergence of quantum
protons, generating a point of incredibly high density known as
a singularity. It could be a rolling area of quantum singularity.
Such a singularity would trigger another big bang. All this being
said, no one can prove that the Big Bang was not triggered by
God.

It seems reasonable that two countervailing forces must exist
in the universe for substantial periods of time to allow oscillation
through the state of co-opetition to occur. Those two countervailing forces are most likely gravity on the one hand versus electromagnetism and the subatomic strong and weak forces on the
other—and scientists are talking about discovering even more
forces.

Is it possible that the quiescent activity of equally balanced
creation and annihilation of matter (virtual particles) and that
antimatter (virtual antiparticles) is the normal state of existence
in the universe—the natural state of space? As said, "quiescence"
is used in this work as a synonym for the state of perfect symmetry of matter and antimatter and the continuing annihilation of
the virtual particles of each. Within its universal realm, quiescence seeks a co-opetitive state.

Under this concept, at a random point in time during quiescence, an aberrant turbulent event may have caused an interruption. That turbulent event theoretically triggered a momentary
imbalance of quiescence. Might that event have ignited a corrective rebalancing process? Was the start of this corrective process, in fact, the Big Bang? Do such disturbances and ensuing big
bangs occur from time to time in the universe?

Studies have shown that given enough time and large enough matrices to work with, spontaneous aberrant events of turbulence or chaos will randomly occur. Recall the famous metaphor of meteorologist Edward Lorenz when he suggested that the flap of a butterfly's wing in Brazil could potentially cause a tornado in Texas. Such occurrences will then give way to correction; that is, to order.

Bibliography

Asaro, V. Frank. *The Tortoise Shell Game.* San Diego: Bettie Youngs Books, 2015.

Badenhousen, Kurt. "The Best States for Business." October 13, 2010. http://www.Forbes.com.

Bateson, Gregory. *Steps to an Ecology of Mind.* Chicago: University of Chicago Press, 2000.

Bernstein, Andrew. *The Capitalist Manifesto: The Historic, Economic, and Philosophic Case for Laissez-Faire.* Lanham, MD: University Press, 2005.

Blanchard, Kenneth, and Spencer Johnson. *The One Minute Manager.* New York: Berkley, 1983.

Boudreaux, Don. "The Great Depression: Myths and Facts." May 5, 2009. http://www.Forbes.com.

Bowles, David. *Building the High-Engagement Work Culture: Balancing "Me" with "We."* New York: Palgrave Macmillan, 2011.

Brown, Daniel James. *The Boys in a Boat.* New York: Penguin Group, 2014.

Calhoun, John B. his rodent studies, Wikipedia

Cox, Jeff, NBC Business News, September 5, 2012.

Diamond, Jared J., PhD. *Guns, Germs and Steel., Collapse: how societies fail or succeed.* 2005 by W.W. Norton & Company.

Family Security Matters.com., *Trump is Right: Illegal Alien Crime is Staggering in Scope and Savagery,* July 10, 2015

Frantz, Roger, and Alex Pattakos (eds.). *Intuition at Work: Pathways to Unlimited Possibilities.* San Francisco, CA: New Leaders Press, 1998.

Friedman, Milton. "How to Cure Health Care." July 30, 2001. *Hoover Digest.*

Ghei, Nita. "Lessons from the Great White North." *Washington Times:* June 11, 2011.

Gibbon, Edward. *The History of the Decline and Fall of the Roman Empire.* London: J. Murray, 1846.

Gillette, Clayton P., Dictatorships for Democracy: Takeovers of Financially Failed Cities, *New York University School of Law,* clayton.gillette@nyu.edu.

Global Research.com-U.S. Military Bases.

Gordon, Claire, "The Real Unemployment Rate is Higher Than You Think." Posted Forbes, April 5th, 2013.

Hampden-Turner, Charles, and Alfons Trompenaars. *The Seven Cultures of Capitalism: Value Systems for Creating Wealth in the United States, Japan, Germany, France, Britain, Sweden, and the Netherlands.* New York: Currency/Doubleday, 1993.

Hannon, Daniel. *The New Road to Serfdom.* Harper Collins, 2010.

Haven, Paul. "Fidel Latest to Say Cuba's Communism Doesn't Work," *Associated Press,* September 9, 2010. http://nl.newsbank.com.

Hock, Dee, speech re chaordic before the Santa Fe Institute, 1993.

Hoover, Kent, "Hey China, Don't Play Chicken With the U.S." *The Business Journal,* August 2 2013.

Kuhn, Harold W. & Sylvia Nasar, *The Essential John Hash,* Princeton, NJ: Princeton University Press, 2007

Laffer, Arthur B. "Taxes, Depression, and Our Current Troubles." *Wall Street Journal.* September 22, 2009.

Levin, Mark. *Liberty and Tyranny.* New York: Threshold Editions, 2010. 27. Levy, Adrian and Cathy-Scott Clark The Man Who Knew Too Much, by, The Guardian, October 13, 2007

Love and Mercy. film. Lions Gate Entertainment and Roadside Attractions, 2015. Writer Oren Moverman, director, Bill Pohlad.

Marlar, Jenny "Gallup-unemployment" *HouseWire*, September 5, 2013

May, Caroline, *93,626 Not In The Labor Force*, Breitbart, June 2, 2015

McCarthy, Ryan. "Greenspan Testifies to Financial Crises Commission, Blames Fannie and Freddie." *Huffington Post*. April 7, 2010.

Meyer, Stephen C., PhD. *Darwin's Doubt*. New York: HarperOne, 2013.

"Microwaves and Plastic Containers." The Canadian Cancer Society. March 11, 2011. http://www.cancer.ca.

Midnight In Paris, Woody Allen produced, directed film, Gravier Productions, et. al.

Morgenson, Gretchen, and Joshua Rosner. *Reckles$ Endangerment: How Outsized Ambition, Greed, and Corruption Led to Economic Armageddon.* New York: Times Books/Henry Holt and Co., 2011.

Nowak, Martin A. "Why We Help: The Evolution of Cooperation," *Scientific American,* June 19, 2012.

O'Brien, John. "Court Revives Reverse-Discrimination Suit against Syracuse Involving Fire Department." *Post-Standard.* August 8, 2010.

Pecastaing, Camille, "The Failure of Democracy and the Rise of the Welfare State," May 3, 2013, *Real ClearPolitics*

Potts, Alex. "Conflict of Interest in Regulatory Reform." April 23, 2010. http://www.Forbes.com.

Powell, Corey S., Have We Found Alien life? Popular Mechanics, Feb. 2015

Quinn, Helen R., and Yossi Nir. *The Mystery of the Missing Antimatter.* Princeton, NJ: Princeton University Press, 2008.

Rand, Ayn. *Atlas Shrugged.* New York: Dutton, 1992.

Ruby Sparks. film directed by Jonathan Dayton, Valerie Faris, written/acted by Zoe Kazan, released by Fox Searchlight Pictures.

Sherk, James. "F.D.R. Warned Us." February 19, 2011. http://www .thefoundry. com.

Sloan, Rick, "Union of Unemployed," The Union of Unemployed.com. March 3, 2013.

Smith, Adam. *An Inquiry into the Nature and Causes of the Wealth of Nations.* Dublin: Whitestone, 1776. ———. *The Theory of Moral Sentiments.* London: A. Strahan, et al., 1792.

"Sweden's Immigration System, Syrian Surge," *Associated Press,* January 30, 2013.

Thompson, William Irwin. *Darkness and Scattered Light: Four Talks on the Future.* Garden City, NY: Anchor Press, 1978.

USA Today, September 10, 2014.

Yahoo Finance, July 2014.

Walker, Scott, Governor Wisconsin; *Unintimidated.* New York:Penguin Group, 2013.

Wall Street 1, 1987 film starring Michel Douglas, directed and co-written by Oliver Stone.

Walters, Ron, *Debate Raged,* Sacramento Bee, April 2015

Ward, Kenric, watchdog.org, August 11, 2014.

"Welfare Reform Turns Ten" Christine Kim and Robert Rector; The Heritage Foundation, 2006.

"World Population in 2300 Could Stabilize at 9 Billion, UN Estimates." *UN News Centre.* November 4, 2004. http://www.un.org.

ABOUT THE AUTHOR

V. Frank Asaro, JD is a lawyer, musician/ composer, inventor and theorist. He authored the non-fiction book, **Universal Co-opetition**, (published October 2011); a novel, **The Tortoise Shell Game**, **(2015)** and now, **A Primal Wisdom, 2D. ED.** (June 2015), the non-fiction corollary to his novel and a 3rd, expanded edition to *Universal Coopetition*. He began developing the theory of co-opetition not long after he was selected out of law school as lawyer-clerk to the California Courts of Appeal. He went on to receive the highest category law career peer review, Preeminent, Martindale Hubbell rating, and has appeared in *Who's Who in American Law*, and *Who's Who in the World*.

Engaged in litigation most of his career, he honed skills proving or disproving facts and stories—a handy talent for a novelist and a theorist. Moreover, as a patent holder, he shows a creative knack. This he calls upon in weaving the most exciting tale of *The*

Tortoise Shell Game, a fiction work in Admiralty law,—one of his fields, and in nailing the theories of this nonfiction corollary, *A Primal Wisdom, 2D. Ed.*. In those early days when he was an Appellate court law clerk, his creativity became a major component in developing the theory of the products liability holding of *Greenman v Yuba Power Products*—further expanded by the California Supreme Court. A major part of the Greenman opinion is now the law in the English speaking and European Union countries of the world.

To offer additional examples of co-opetition, or to contact the author, in general:

www.vfrankasaroauthor.com

or

info@vfrankasaroauthor.com.

Also by V Frank Asaro

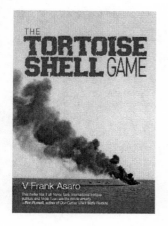

The Tortoise Shell Game

Off the coast of Central America, the *Sea Diva*, a tuna boat, sinks. Members of the crew are missing and what happened remains a mystery. Anthony Darren, a renowned and wealthy lawyer at the top of his game, knows the boat's owner and soon becomes involved in the case. As the case goes to trial, a missing crew member is believed to be at fault, but new evidence comes to light and the finger of guilt points in a completely unanticipated direction.

Now Anthony must pull together all his resources to find the truth in what has happened and free a wrongly accused man— as well as untangle himself. Fighting despair, he finds that the recent events have called much larger issues into question. As he struggles to right this terrible wrong, Anthony makes new and enlightening discoveries in his own life-long battle for personal and global justice.

ISBN 978-1-940784-49-6

eBook ISBN: 978-1-940784-50-2

Thriller / Fiction • $25.95

Also:
Althea Haunting
A 2016 Release

Bettie Youngs Books

We specialize in MEMOIRS
. . . books that celebrate
fascinating people and
remarkable journeys

CPSIA information can be obtained
at www.ICGtesting.com
Printed in the USA
FSOW01n1545080816
23557FS